STOP SELLING *and* START LISTENING!

Marketing Strategies That Create Top Producers

By
Chip Cummings, CMC

Northwind Publishing
Grand Rapids, Michigan
www.StopSellingAndStartListening.com

Stop Selling and Start Listening
Marketing Strategies That Create Top Producers

By Chip Cummings, CMC

Northwind Financial Corporation
Northwind Publishing
Grand Rapids, Michigan
www.NorthwindFinancial.com

Printed and bound in the United States of America

This book is available at quantity discounts for bulk purchases by organizations, businesses and associations. For more information, or to find out about speaking/training availability, please contact the publisher.

ISBN   0-9746975-1-6

Cover Illustration: Archer-Ellison
Interior Design: Heather Kirk, www.BrandedForSuccess.com
Illustrations: Megan Johnson
Editors: Doug Florzak; Debra Forth

3rd Printing

This book is dedicated to my wife Lisa –
as my best friend, the love of my life,
#1 supporter, and mother to my
three precious kids – Katelyn, CJ and Joe
(who have taught us the art of listening!)

What Others Are Saying...

Chip Cummings' masterful Stop Selling and Start Listening *is so good that even the title gives you a running start. The book is crammed with crucial insights and valuable tips that will have a positive impact upon your earnings. All that, and it's a lot of fun to read, too. I believe it should be required reading for anyone in the world of sales and marketing.*

~Jay Conrad Levinson, The Father of Guerrilla Marketing
Author, *Guerrilla Marketing* series of books, over 14 million sold; now in 41 languages
www.GMarketing.com, www.GuerrillaMarketingAssociation.com

The Sweet Truth about the most important component of any business plan... MARKETING! Stop Selling and Start Listening *masterfully blends the cerebral insights necessary for attracting the customers that we all want, with proven and practical applications on how to make the most out of your marketing dollars.*

~ Tim Braheem, Founder and CEO – The Loan Toolbox
www.LoanToolbox.com

Stop Selling and Start Listening *is a must read for anyone serious about success in selling. Chip Cummings' easy to read "How-to" manual, offers concrete, sure-fire suggestions for turning prospects into customers. No matter how many years you've been at it — from novice to top producer — this book should be required reading. Be sure to read it before your next sales presentation.*

~ Sig Anderman, CEO, Ellie Mae, Inc.

Incredible material — Chip's techniques have had a dramatic impact on my business, and I would recommend this book to any business owner or sales professional.

~ Les Brown, International Motivational Speaker and Best-Selling Author of
Live Your Dreams, It's Not Over 'til You Win, and *Up Thoughts for Down Times*

"This is an incredible book by Chip Cummings! The information in this book will make the sales side of any business more professional, credible and respectable with its real-time and cutting edge strategies. Chip has masterfully covered everything one needs to know to master the sales process. Anyone serious about their business and taking their career to world class levels must embrace this information and take action. The ultimate beneficiary of this book will be the customer!"

~ Mike Baker, Founder/CEO of LoanOfficerStore.com
Author, Speaker and Trainer

Acknowledgements

Putting a book together is a lot of work! If it weren't for the help of many key individuals, this project never would have seen the light of day. I want to express my extreme gratitude to the following friends and associates, without whom, I never would have had the opportunity to learn, grow and share my experiences. It's through all of you that I continue to explore new strategies – and enjoy the challenges and blessings presented to me each and every day.

First, I want to thank God for the gifts and opportunities provided to me, and for allowing me to lead a purpose driven life! Special thanks to Debbie Forth – my assistant and right arm, who keeps me organized and runs the show! To Les Brown for your guidance, friendship, and dedication to bettering the lives of millions around world – you continue to amaze and inspire me. Mike Williams for your wisdom and common-sense guidance: 3 questions, right?

Jay Conrad Levinson, you are a true pioneer and "guerilla", and it's an honor to be your "student!" To Fred Gleeck, thanks for your insights and constantly pushing me to "think big" – theatre in New York will never be the same! To my editors and designer, Doug Florzak and Heather Kirk, thanks for your patience and hanging in there to make sure it got done right. And to my bro Ken, Mr. Ultimate – the Bob Vila of the graphics world, for your love and support.

To my friends and associates Alex Mandossian, Rick Raddatz and Armand Morin for sharing your ideas, expertise and shortening the learning curve. To Jody and Tom Kinney for patience, love and guidance of the future "hall-of-famer." Kevin Bracy – your energy and message is truly infectious – let's do

For a FREE 7-day course on "7 Steps To Building A Successful Marketing Plan," send an e-mail to ChipTips@ChipCummings.com

i

London again soon! To Heidi, Mark and the whole gang at The Office – it's gonna be fun!

Tim Braheem, Mike Baker (Mr. Trust and Credibility), Dave Hershman and Doug Smith – you guys inspire and push me to concentrate on delivering quality stuff, and it's a pleasure to work with you.

Thanks to friend and attorney Mark Rabidoux of Trott & Trott, PC for your valuable insight and input, the Board of the MMBA – especially Tim Kleyla and Dave Acquisti for your support and the opportunity to be a part of the vision, and Ruth Faynor and Bill Pape for your stories and contributions.

Finally, a special thanks to all my former and current employees, and to the hundreds upon hundreds of loan officers, sales professionals and business owners who have shared their successes and struggles, and allowed me to be a part of their world – you make it fun to come to work everyday!

For a FREE 7-day course on "7 Steps To Building A Successful Marketing Plan," send an e-mail to ChipTips@ChipCummings.com

ii

Chip's Notes

Well, here it is… thanks to the help of literally hundreds of people! I enjoy the world of sales, and more than that I enjoy helping people with creative ways to accelerate their sales careers and businesses. It is my hope that you will find some clever ideas to implement in your operation that will allow you to attract and capture new customers, and better understand the process of how to become a Top Producer. It doesn't happen by accident.

I have included several "Chip Tips" at the end of each chapter to highlight each of the important points and strategies discussed, with specific tools and resources that I use on a regular basis for my own business operations, and those of my consulting clients from around the world.

Take these ideas and concepts — use them and mold them to fit your personal business plan. Then let me know about your success! Come and find me at one of the many events I am at, or drop me a line anytime. You can do it — the tools are available, the roadmap has been laid out. You just need to make the decision to be bold and follow your dreams. It won't be easy, and it will take some time. People will look at you strange at times, but that's because there aren't many people enjoying the level of success you're after – but it's worth the trip.

Remember that success is not a destination — it's the journey itself. It's not about you. There are many people to help you on your journey, you just need to learn to listen to them!

For a FREE 7-day course on "7 Steps To Building A Successful Marketing Plan," send an e-mail to ChipTips@ChipCummings.com

iii

This book is designed to help you learn and profit using certain marketing concepts and strategies. While all information was checked for accuracy at time of publication, website addresses, links and companies are bound to change.

I have personally used and continue to use the strategies and techniques discussed in this book. I make no claims, guarantees or predictions as to your personal success, as that depends entirely upon you and your abilities and resources. If you do find any errors in this book, they are here for a purpose. Some people actually like looking for them and we strive to please as many people as possible! If you find any typos, or encounter problems with any links or information, please send me an e-mail at info@ChipCummings.com so we can research it, get you the corrected info, and update it for future editions. If you send me a number of them, I will reward you with a small gift – unless you find so many of them that I feel you deserve a large gift!

Thanks for reading, now go forth and profit!

For a FREE 7-day course on "7 Steps To Building A Successful Marketing Plan," send an e-mail to ChipTips@ChipCummings.com

iv

Foreword

To Professional Salespeople All Over The World,

With the mindset of a successful entrepreneur, top sales professional and dynamic speaker, Chip Cummings, using everyday language, shares with us cutting edge strategies on how to effectively connect with our customers, dramatically increase our sales and experientially grow our profits.

Pulling from his experiences of creating and operating numerous businesses starting from childhood selling rocks with his playmates to their neighbors, Chip provides simple yet profound methods you can apply right now by paying more attention to what your customers are saying.

As you read each chapter, lights will come on. What he writes is common sense but not common practice. In the highly competitive and complicated marketplace, most people focus on doing more selling and simply hope the customers buy. Chip wisely instructs us to stop selling, and to start listening, and that that will give you the opportunity to provide more value, create deeper relationships and create customers for life.

By keeping an ear on the pulse of the marketplace it allows you to maintain a constant presence in the minds of your customers. Einstein said genius is having the capacity to take the complicated and make it simple. Chip believes that whatever frustrates you is the key to your success. I'm sure there are many people like myself who find today's rapidly changing technology complicated and frustrating. In this book, Chip decodes, de-mystifies, and walks you through the process on how to create and apply innovative customer centric methods like a pro.

For a FREE 7-day course on "7 Steps To Building A Successful Marketing Plan," send an e-mail to ChipTips@ChipCummings.com

v

It's been an honor to share the platform with him and watch him with passion, enlighten and empower audiences. I feel blessed to have him as a friend and a business coach. I'm positive you will see your life and business with new eyes after reading this book. I strongly advise you to listen well.

Chip, you've made me proud!

~ Les Brown

International Motivational Speaker, and Best-Selling Author of Live Your Dreams, It's Not Over 'til You Win, *and* Up Thoughts for Down Times

For a FREE 7-day course on "7 Steps To Building A Successful Marketing Plan," send an e-mail to ChipTips@ChipCummings.com

vi

Contents

For a FREE 7-day course on "7 Steps To Building A Successful Marketing Plan," send an e-mail to ChipTips@ChipCummings.com

1

For a FREE 7-day course on "7 Steps To Building A Successful Marketing Plan," send an e-mail to ChipTips@ChipCummings.com

2

Chapter 1

Marketing: The Million Dollar Journey

"The only thing consistent in this business is change."

Chip Cummings

There are people who make things happen, those who watch things happen, and those who wonder... "What happened?" If you are still trying to reach customers the same way you did three years ago, you could be part of the group wondering — what happened.

Thanks to technology, our world changes at a very rapid pace. The way we shop, the way we compare products and services, how we research and gather information — the whole way we communicate and reach people has shifted dramatically.

While the world changes, the basic principals of marketing stay the same.

I have the privilege to speak and work with sales professionals daily — thousands over the past several years. No matter where I go, people across the country ask the same questions: "What does it take to be successful? What do Top Producers do differently that dramatically sets them apart from everyone else?"

Why is it that some people struggle for years, yet others — relative newcomers — can achieve seemingly "overnight"

For a FREE 7-day course on "7 Steps To Building A Successful Marketing Plan," send an e-mail to ChipTips@ChipCummings.com

3

superstar status? Well, the answers are not as elusive or difficult as you might imagine. Just as it takes a certain combination of ingredients to bake the perfect cake, so it goes with becoming a superstar salesperson. There is nothing special about ordinary flour, sugar, eggs and baking soda — but you put them all together in just the right way, add a little heat, and presto! Fortunately, we can narrow your personal recipe for success down to seven basic ingredients.

The Recipe of Success

While there may be seven key ingredients in the makeup of a Top Producer, research has shown that no matter what product or service you provide — your long-term success, or the recipe itself, always boils down to marketing. You can have the best restaurant in town or the fastest package delivery service in the world, but if no one knows about it, it just remains a well kept secret. But you have to have the right target, right message, right timing, and the right mixture of everything. Just like an award-winning secret chili recipe, Top Producers have figured out how to "mix just the right ingredients" to create a formula for success.

But what exactly is marketing? Marketing is *listening* to your customers' problems — and offering the right solution, to the right audience, at the right time, under just the right circumstances. Sounds simple, right? Let me try to simplify it a little more —

Marketing is the art of putting yourself directly
in the path of an interested, qualified customer.

It differs from Sales. Sales is a much more proactive approach — searching for qualified customers and then trying to get them interested in your product or service. Marketing

For a FREE 7-day course on "7 Steps To Building A Successful Marketing Plan," send an e-mail to ChipTips@ChipCummings.com

4

attracts peoples' attention and defines what you do, such that people who approach you are already pre-selected to be good candidates for your product or service. *Targeted* marketing makes your "sale" easier because your potential customers are pre-sold before they arrive at your door. *Integrated* marketing is the strategy that ties all of your efforts together to reach prospects in multiple ways while producing a single unified message. The engine's just not as effective when 2 of the cylinders are misfiring — even by just a little bit.

So how do we develop a successful, integrated, targeted marketing strategy in such a rapidly changing marketplace?

What *you will learn in this book* are specific methods and techniques that I successfully use, which help companies and individuals attract new customers, capture leads, increase their business, and retain long-lasting clients. You will discover what creates Top Producers — how they think, create, plan and execute. You will learn how they play the game — *and how they win*.

The $1,000,000 Journey

To get you started, think for a couple of minutes about what I call the million dollar question.

Pretend that I blindfold and transport you to some strange city. As I uncover your eyes, I explain to you there is one million dollars sitting in a chest at the corner of Washington Ave. and Sixteenth Street. The money is in a green box that can only be opened with this special key I'm handing you. Could you find it with just this limited amount of information? How hard would you try? I hope you said "if there's a million dollars waiting for me, I'd sure as heck figure it out. I'll track down every Washington and Sixteenth Street I can find in the entire country!"

For a FREE 7-day course on "7 Steps To Building A Successful Marketing Plan," send an e-mail to ChipTips@ChipCummings.com

5

That's the idea, but wait — I said nothing about this intersection even being in any particular country.

Maybe you need to learn a bit more information. Suppose I share with you the knowledge that Interstate-10 runs through this town. Now we are sure the intersection is in the United States at least. Your next step would likely be to secure a map and find every city along I-10 where that intersection might be located. Okay — so far, so good.

But the path to your riches is still difficult to plot. You may be shaking your head, saying, "I'm having a hard time figuring this out." Okay — I'll give you another clue: Sky Harbor International Airport. With a minimal amount of research, you would quickly discover that Sky Harbor airport is located in Phoenix, Arizona.

To understand the secrets of successful marketing, you have to understand this scenario because locating customers is very similar. Top producers know how to mix the seven key ingredients to navigate the route faster, avoid roadblocks, drive with blinders on — and enjoy every step of the journey. Each piece of information I supply you, makes it clearer how to reach that million dollar goal. There is always a period of uncertainty about where your path will lead you, and, to make matters worse, in the real world, your customers will periodically move or even disguise the box!

Now that you figured out the city, you get excited. You jump in the car and start to speed down the road. "Wait a minute — where am I?" Great Question! To get from where you are to ANY goal, it is *equally important to discover exactly where you are* at the start of the journey.

This is a *critical factor that most salespeople don't take the time to figure out* — where they are right now. Think about an alcoholic.

For a FREE 7-day course on "7 Steps To Building A Successful Marketing Plan," send an e-mail to ChipTips@ChipCummings.com

6

Until they admit their problem, that person can not begin to break out of their negative situation. Being honest about their starting point is the key to their potential success.

You know you want more customers, but until you clearly understand exactly where you are, you can't know which direction to travel to find them. This book will help you define where you are, point you in the right direction, and teach you to build a personal and professional roadmap to success.

✦

Back on your quest for the Million Dollars, you suddenly see why figuring out your starting place is so critical. To get to Phoenix, you must figure out if I relocated you to a city that is north, south, east or west of that location.

A quick analysis of your surroundings shows you are in the United States — in Detroit, Michigan. You search for a U.S. map and plot your course. You will pass through Chicago, St Louis, Kansas City, Oklahoma City, Dallas and then southwest to Phoenix. That is the quickest route to drive. Or is it?

As you begin your journey, you power up the radio to listen to the weather and traffic reports. Almost immediately, you hear that a bridge on your route through Chicago has collapsed. You consult your map and devise a detour around the city to avoid the delays. As you approach St. Louis, you hear that, about the time you estimate your arrival in Kansas City, they are expecting a series of tornados to strike the area.

You study your map again. Knowing where you are now, you decide to drop south to Little Rock and then over to Oklahoma City. As you reach the edge of Oklahoma's capital,

For a FREE 7-day course on "7 Steps To Building A Successful Marketing Plan," send an e-mail to ChipTips@ChipCummings.com

7

radio reports indicate major flooding is taking place in the Dallas area. Once again, because you are certain about your current location, the map shows that you can go straight west to New Mexico before turning southwest toward Phoenix.

Finally, after several changes in your original plans, you arrive at Washington Ave. and Sixteenth Street. The box with your Million Dollars is there and you collect it!

Enjoying the Trip

When you look back, it almost seems funny. The long difficult trip took a lot of time and effort, but you made it. First you had to clarify exactly what the goal was, and then be honest about your current situation, or location. Next, you plotted your fastest route and began your journey. You drove a car, but others may have decided to fly, take a train, and some may even have chosen to walk! What you learned along the way is that obstacles continually arise. As long as you remained focused on your destination, you learned to find alternate paths that kept you moving toward your goal. No matter how large the obstacle, or how bad the circumstances, the dream of that reward enriching the quality of your life

For a FREE 7-day course on "7 Steps To Building A Successful Marketing Plan," send an e-mail to ChipTips@ChipCummings.com

8

made every adjustment — although frustrating at times — worth the detours and delays. That is the road to success.

Marketing is the vehicle, the fuel, and the adventure. Start by being honest about your current efforts. Set measurable, reachable intermediate destinations and don't let anything stop you. If one path closes, another path opens. *The creativity and flexibility to change course when necessary, and the ability to remain focused on your direction, are your greatest allies.*

But while the road to success may be paved with good intentions, it falls apart without the presence of two key ingredients — Value and Belief. These are the two important fuels that keep you going. You must place a high personal value on the destination, and also have an unshakeable belief that you can get there. In our example we used a million dollars to symbolize the value, but our goal could just as easily have been to retire early, buy a new house, put your kids through college, spend more time with your family or whatever is important to you. To complete that journey, you also had to believe that the destination exists — that the reward at the end of your journey was worth obtaining.

Without the fuel of both Value and Belief feeding your vehicle, it is hard to enjoy the trip. There are bumps, bruises and delays along the route — and many people just run out of gas and give up. If you couldn't picture the reward, and thus believe in the value to you at the end, it would be too easy to quit.

Without a focused destination — well, ANY road will take you somewhere eventually — but it sure won't serve up the same reward! You will wander around until frustration forces you to take another look at the map.

Too often, "personal detours" lead you down the wrong road. Even with detailed directions and recognizable landmarks, dozens of "excuses" are waiting to slow you down. Detours

For a FREE 7-day course on "7 Steps To Building A Successful Marketing Plan," send an e-mail to ChipTips@ChipCummings.com

9

constantly show up in the form of fear (both fear of failure and fear of success), lack of practical experience or education, the distractions of life, greed, laziness, or sometimes — irrational optimism! Often, people get defeated by their own stubbornness. Once in a while on a journey, you will find a grand canyon. Too often, people optimistically cling to the hope that they can somehow find a way to jump over it, when in reality it would be wiser to go around.

Everyone's got a "personal detour" as an excuse not to succeed. What's yours? By the end of this book, you will learn how to recognize these detours — not that you can avoid them, but rather to minimize the delay they have on your ultimate journey.

Through this journey, you will learn how to listen. Listen for the sounds of your own engine, the sounds of your surroundings, and the sounds of your customers. You'll discover how to hear the sound of success. The further down the road you go, the better equipped you'll be to handle the detours.

Remember the Million Dollar journey. Forget about where you've been — where are you RIGHT NOW? Where do you want to go? What's the value to you? Do you believe the reward is worth the trip? I KNOW you can get there — you just have to take the first step.

So start your engine, and get ready. Your personal Million Dollar journey begins now.

For a FREE 7-day course on "7 Steps To Building A Successful Marketing Plan," send an e-mail to ChipTips@ChipCummings.com

10

Chapter 2

The Anatomy of a Customer

"There is only one marketing genius, and that's the customer."
Chip Cummings

"Don't spend major time with minor people"
George Fraser

There is only one person that gets to decide if your marketing strategies work — the customer. The customer is King, and companies spend millions of dollars trying to figure out how to position themselves directly in front of the Throne.

Since you don't have a multi-million dollar advertising budget and dozens of analysts carefully calculating market position and consumer trends, you can't afford marketing by trial-and-error! Before we can start mapping out your marketing plan, we need to cover some basic "rules of the road", and understand what makes up a customer — and then, if it's possible to predict what they might do.

Predictable Consistency

Like any profession, Marketing has rules. A true craftsperson knows the rules in their field. Once they understand the guidelines

For a FREE 7-day course on "7 Steps To Building A Successful Marketing Plan," send an e-mail to ChipTips@ChipCummings.com

11

in which they operate, they accept when they need to adhere to those rules, and when they can creatively bend or even break them.

Learn the basic rules of marketing.

Consistency is the foundation. Customers like consistency, or they get confused, and a confused mind says "no". Our overall efficiency and profits go up when customers react in a predictable pattern, so our marketing success must be built on achieving consistent results. If we can predict HOW potential customers will react to certain messages, then we can measure the consistency of that reaction, and subsequently better control our market, profits, and our success.

If I asked you to pick up an object, hold it away from your body, then open your thumb and fingers, we both know that the item would fall to the ground. Anywhere on the planet, the result is the same. This is the unbreakable "Law of Gravity." We have learned from a very early age, that every time we repeat the experiment by jumping off the bed or the roof of the house, we would get same result, 100% of the time. That's consistency!

If instead, I ask you to throw that object to a friend; we know that human nature dictates that they are going to attempt to catch it. That is a different action. Many variables come into play. Sometimes he'll catch it, and sometimes he might drop it. If he is not looking or I throw it too fast, it might bounce off his hands and bang into the wall. While we can't predict what will happen 100% of the time, we can develop a reaction model that I call *"predictable consistency."* That is to say, if we have his attention, and we throw it the same way each time, we know that he will catch it 90 to 95% of the time!

The same effect is true in marketing, and Top Producers know this. If we can develop strategies that can consistently predict how a potential customer will react, then we just need to do it repetitively until the reaction changes.

For a FREE 7-day course on "7 Steps To Building A Successful Marketing Plan," send an e-mail to ChipTips@ChipCummings.com

12

While some rules in marketing are consistent, others you may need to adapt to a particular time and place. So how do we determine what the customer wants? Or better yet, how do *we encourage them to figure out that what we have is what they want*? By actively listening to what they're saying, and then reacting with a consistent message.

The Four Food Groups

A good place to start in understanding the listening process is to examine the anatomy of a customer. What are they thinking? How do they act or react? How do I approach them? When do I close? How do I open? What exactly influences a potential client? Let's begin with what I call "The Four Food Groups." Everyone out there falls into one of four categories: Suspects, Prospects, Customers (or Clients), or Evangelists.

They all start out as part of the first group, and the idea is to move them along our success cycle from left to right as follows:

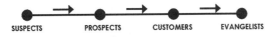

SUSPECTS   PROSPECTS   CUSTOMERS   EVANGELISTS

Suspects

By far the largest of the groups, the "Suspects" include anyone who might have a use for your products or service at any time in the future. They may need you next week, next year, or maybe not for 15 years, but at some point they will be in the market. The Nike company understands the power of capturing this market early. Although the typical 8-year old doesn't need a $100 pair of running shoes, they will most certainly recognize the "swoosh" by the time they graduate years later, then head for the sports shop, where they will pay for performance.

For a FREE 7-day course on "7 Steps To Building A Successful Marketing Plan," send an e-mail to ChipTips@ChipCummings.com

13

But, we're not competing on the same level as a "Nike". Most salespeople spend the majority of their energy on the Suspects, trying to get them to move into the next group — the "Prospects". The inexperienced salesperson works furiously, searching for any lead, saying to themselves "It's a numbers game." No it's not! There are lots of roads out there, but I'm only interested in the one's that will take me in the direction I'm going! As you will see, Top Producers know that this group is where you will spend the least amount of your time and energy.

Prospects

Suspects turn into Prospects as soon as they express any kind of interest in your products or services, or when you can readily identify an immediate need. If you own a restaurant, Prospects start to show up when they get hungry. But you must also learn to recognize an "unconscious" need, similar to when someone decides to buy a new home. They may not know it yet, but they will need financing, homeowners insurance, an appraisal, title search, and a host of other services. For marketing purposes, both the conscience and unconscious Prospects can be easily targeted as well.

Once an interest or need is identified or established, there are 4 "stages of readiness" that Prospects go through before they can get to the next group and become customers. These four stages are the "Not Now", "Not Yet", "Maybe", and "Ready" people. Not all Prospects will be ready at the same time, and many may not reach a point where your product or service is relevant to them for quite awhile! You need to listen in order to recognize which phase they're in, or you could be wasting time and energy selling them on something they're not ready for.

The "Not Now" group is too preoccupied with other priorities to even listen to you, let alone act on a decision.

For a FREE 7-day course on "7 Steps To Building A Successful Marketing Plan," send an e-mail to ChipTips@ChipCummings.com

14

They know that they will eventually need an insurance agent, but that's of minor importance when they haven't even talked to a real estate agent yet!

The "Not Yet" clan has noticed advertisements and starts to pay attention to what their friends are saying about the local housing market conditions, but they're still looking "down the road." Their need has just started to creep into the conscious mind, and although not urgent, they'll "let you know" or will "be in touch." This is a critical stage for you, as this is where the relationship-building period starts. DON'T PUSH! Inexperienced salespeople tend to call persistently or "close" too early, which only offends the Prospect and builds an uncomfortable wall that is hard to tear down.

Now, the "Maybe" group is fully conscious of their need, but is still shopping — albeit more actively. This is the best phase to clearly identify the "Personal Value" that you bring to the transaction. We will spend a considerable amount of time in Chapter 4 identifying how to position yourself to take advantage of this group *before* the competition gets the opportunity to. This phase is where trust-building strategies become crucial.

Before you can move a Prospect forward, you need to understand another basic rule of marketing:

People only do business with people that they trust, and they only trust people that they like.

They will only "like" you when they feel you clearly understand their needs and priorities, and treat them with GREATER importance than your needs and priorities.

Finally, a Prospect will move into the "Ready" mode. They now understand the need, understand your solution, and are

For a FREE 7-day course on "7 Steps To Building A Successful Marketing Plan," send an e-mail to ChipTips@ChipCummings.com

15

comfortable trusting you to attend to their priorities. I have heard many "sales experts" say that to be successful at selling, you need to "close early and close often." That approach may get you the sale faster, but it will be at the expense of the long-term relationship. If the customer hasn't reached the "Ready" stage, all this approach will do is brand you as a "Salesman" — not as a valued consultant or trusted advisor. If you have handled these stages correctly, the customer will *move themselves* to the next stage: Customer.

Customers

The third group on the success timeline are our Customers (or Clients). A customer can be defined as anyone who has signed an agreement, made some type of personal commitment or spent at least $1 with you. This group justifiably requires more time from us, but not in the way most salespeople tend to spend it. Inexperienced salespeople merely service the immediate needs of the customer. Top Producers attack this stage as an opportunity to reinforce the customers' decision for a long-term relationship, and to establish the groundwork that leads them into the final magical group: Evangelists.

Evangelists

This is the "Holy Grail" for Top Producers. The average salesperson stops working at the Customer stage, but *Top Producers spend most of their time and energy devoted to this category*. They recognize the importance of creating a "Wow!" experience to develop customers who become "walking billboards", and then evangelize their experience to their friends, coworkers, neighbors, strangers, and anyone within a 30-mile radius of where they're standing!

For a FREE 7-day course on "7 Steps To Building A Successful Marketing Plan," send an e-mail to ChipTips@ChipCummings.com

16

While it takes more effort and planning to get people to this stage, this is where long-term success is defined. On average, an estimated 82% of all your profits will come as a direct result of the people in this category. Listen to their experiences! Treat them well, and they will do the same for you.

Learn To Ask Questions!

So now that we understand the different phases that our Suspects have to go through, how exactly do we identify which stage they're in — and when they're ready to move on? The best way is to ask questions and listen! Asking questions provides an objective look at their wants and needs, and experienced listening becomes your most powerful tool.

I'm not talking about a simple observation such as "They need to eat so I'm going sell them food." It doesn't work that way. Instead, you need to ask yourself, "Since I know they get hungry, how can I offer inviting selections to increase the likelihood they will pick one of my selections?"

It is not cost effective for me to search aimlessly for potential customers wandering around lost and hungry (Suspects). It makes more sense to position my menu choices to hungry people who can then make a decision to pick my restaurant and spend their money (Prospects).

Asking questions is the most effective way to figure out what they want. From there, determine what their needs are. Quite often, suspects and prospects are not going to know or clearly understand their needs. That's where the "listening" comes in, as one of the vital areas in analyzing and developing a successful marketing strategy.

In order to capitalize on this hidden need, listen to what their conscious mind says, but *sell to the unconscious mind.* People

For a FREE 7-day course on "7 Steps To Building A Successful Marketing Plan," send an e-mail to ChipTips@ChipCummings.com

17

primarily make purchasing decisions from an emotional standpoint, but they need to justify that purchase with logic.

Hear what they "say" they want, and figure out the solutions you have that fit that need — not only their perceived need, but their actual need.

I have met with tens of thousands of clients during my 20+ years involved in financing real estate transactions, and have racked up over a billion dollars is sales volume. If you ask clients to verbalize what they needed, the response was always the same: money to finance a home. But that wasn't the entire answer. I can safely say that with all those transactions over the years, no two were ever the same. Sure there were similarities, but the puzzle pieces always went together a little differently for each deal.

While the basic end objective could be viewed as a need for money, only by asking a series of carefully structured questions and practicing intelligent listening, was I able to truly figure out the motivation *behind* the transaction, and come up with the right combination of terms, payments, costs, and then produce a strategy that would be beneficial in creating a long-term happy client. Forgetting to ask a critical question, or assuming I already knew the answer, could have meant serious financial repercussions for them down the road, not only resulting in a loss of that customer, but access to their personal contacts and future referrals as well!

The 3-Part Throne

Even though the Customer is King, there are certain rules *they* must live with as well. There are 3 critical elements that go into any and every transaction. It makes no difference if you're selling mortgages, insurance, hotdogs, furniture, cars, or books. There are always three components that go into the sales equation: price, quality, and service.

For a FREE 7-day course on "7 Steps To Building A Successful Marketing Plan," send an e-mail to ChipTips@ChipCummings.com

18

The basic "Law of Economics" states that you can deliver two out of the three; but you can never provide all three simultaneously. You can provide service and quality, but you're going to forego price, because quality components and great service are going to be more expensive.

You can deliver great service at a nice price, but you're going to forego quality. That's like comparing a Chevy subcompact to a Rolls Royce. The Chevy has a better price and offers great service but it's certainly not the quality of a Rolls.

You can say, "I'll sell you top quality at the best price" but then you can't afford to provide a high level of service. There are a lot of Internet sales that follow this model.

The reason you cannot provide all three simultaneously is that you will go broke! That's a rule of marketing. If you are constantly looking to attract customers with price alone, you need to decide which one you are willing to compromise on — quality or service? Of course, anyone providing only *one* of the three will not last in the marketplace very long!

In most sales transactions involving any type of professional service, price is the one that needs to be "dropped" — but again, the inexperienced salesperson will usually decide that price is all too important. They lower it to get the sale, yet still strive to provide all three elements, just to become exhausted and broke!

In my industry of real estate mortgage lending, the most common question from a prospect is, "What's your interest rate today?" Unfortunately, this is how we have trained the public to shop — by interest rate alone. They don't know what other questions to ask! Worse yet, most mortgage loan officers give a direct answer and quote a rate! Wrong thing to do. You cannot sell price alone in that industry, because there is ALWAYS someone who will beat you on price.

For a FREE 7-day course on "7 Steps To Building A Successful Marketing Plan," send an e-mail to ChipTips@ChipCummings.com

19

In that situation, my favorite answer to give a Prospect is, "What do you want your interest rate to be?" Confused, they typically respond, "Huh? I just called 20 people out of the phonebook to find out what their interest rates are, and you're going to let me pick the interest rate that I want. Why?" It completely takes them off guard, and re-focuses the conversation where I want it to go — to service and quality.

It opens up their mind to other possibilities. They are used to hearing somebody say, "Oh, it's six percent" or "It's six and a half percent." Once I divert their attention, I take it a step further, saying "I can give you a rate of 1 1/4%, but to get that low rate there are tradeoffs that might not be in your best interest. Tell me more about your situation, and then I can explain how you can obtain the most cost-effective rate and terms for your situation, and we can make a much more intelligent long-term financial decision."

I've taken the Price element right off the table! They have quickly learned that "the best rate" (price) might do them more harm than good.

I win customers over, and earn the right to do business with them if they feel I'm sincerely committed to making sure they get what they need, with a solution that makes economic sense for their specific situation. Their needs are more important than mine.

The same is true for ANY type of business. When you get a potential client in the door, help them understand that price is not necessarily the thing that they want to be looking for. There is a certain quality and service that outweighs the price that they're going to pay.

Yes, price does matter, but not with the same importance. I'm always going to be reasonably priced, but I've chosen not to be the Rolls Royce of my business and charge for all sorts of extras. You must evaluate where you stand in your industry. Remember

For a FREE 7-day course on "7 Steps To Building A Successful Marketing Plan," send an e-mail to ChipTips@ChipCummings.com

20

our Million Dollar journey? Before you begin to market yourself and your services or products, you must define where you are and who you are. Are you going to be in the economy, mid-level or the "Rolls-Royce" category? In Chapter 4 — The Rule of Reality, we will walk through an eye-opening exercise that will help you decide just that.

The "Chip Value"

In almost all sales transactions, customers don't mind paying a fair price for quality products and services (and the ones who do mind, you don't want as customers anyway!) I make sure my clients understand there is a certain expertise, or "Chip Value" that I bring to every transaction. There is a certain service that I, Chip Cummings, bring to the table and that they can't get anywhere else. Anyone can sell a pair of shoes, but few do it with the style and attention of Nordstrom's. I help them to understand and appreciate why my "Personal Value" is far more important than mere price.

◆

Take the time to understand what phase the potential customer is in, what their true needs are, and how you can satisfy that need beyond price, by introducing your own Personal Value. Successful selling centered around Quality and Service is based on establishing the relationship before the sale — not after.

Remember — People trust people they like. If a customer isn't fond of you, they are less likely to do business with you. Even if you *do* induce them into a working relationship, you may regret the results. They are not going to give you referrals, testimonials, or ever come back again, if they don't grow to like you — they have too many other choices in the marketplace.

For a FREE 7-day course on "7 Steps To Building A Successful Marketing Plan," send an e-mail to ChipTips@ChipCummings.com

21

Make very sure you understand your customer's needs, and then respond to them on their terms to ensure you become "business friends." Once you have established that connection on a personal level, they trust you. Only then, do you have a chance at obtaining repeat business with those customers.

There is a wise, old axiom: Customers don't care how much you know, until they know how much you care. Take this to heart, and listen to them carefully. Treat them with respect and they will reward you with loyalty. Your competition is out there marketing for the sale — you need to be marketing for the relationship.

The 3 Critical Questions

Knowing what makes a customer "tick" is the easy part. Several chapters in this book will deal with the more difficult strategies of developing a roadmap for driving customers through the business cycle and learning how to ask exactly the right questions. But before we can start on our Million Dollar Journey, we've got a few tough questions that need to be answered about ourselves.

No matter what your product or service, every Suspect in the marketplace will want an answer to these three critical questions before they consider doing business with you. The three key questions are:

✦ Who are you?

✦ What have you got? and

✦ Why should I care?

Let's start with the first one, and look at what are the critical ingredients that go into creating a "Top Producer."

For a FREE 7-day course on "7 Steps To Building A Successful Marketing Plan," send an e-mail to ChipTips@ChipCummings.com

22

CHIP TIPS:

Here are your "personal road signs" from this Chapter:

1. Learn the basic "Rules of Marketing"

2. Understand the concept of "Predictable Consistency" and how potential customers will react in the marketplace

3. Learn to recognize how people fit into the four food groups — Suspects; Prospects; Customers; and Evangelists

4. Learn to ask questions, how to listen for the answers, and interpret the reactions

5. Remember that people only do business with people that they trust, and only trust people they like — build the relationship *before* the sale

6. Be prepared to answer the three critical questions — Who Are You, What Have You Got, and Why Should I Care?

For a FREE 7-day course on "7 Steps To Building A Successful Marketing Plan," send an e-mail to ChipTips@ChipCummings.com

23

For a FREE 7-day course on "7 Steps To Building A Successful Marketing Plan," send an e-mail to ChipTips@ChipCummings.com

24

Chapter 3

What Makes Up a Top Producer?

"There are two kinds of people, those who do the work and those who take credit. Try and be in the first group; there is less competition there."

Indira Gandhi

You've heard people say it a thousand times — "He's a natural born salesperson" or "He was born to sell." It's as if they believe top sales producers were given a genetic "leg up" in the same way Michael Jordan was born with certain advantages to play basketball. Hogwash!

I don't believe this. Unlike basketball, where some natural-born talent is the minimum admission to a professional sports career, selling is a learned skill. In other words, Top Producers don't have better genes than you — they have just learned and developed more effective habits.

Successful Habits of Top Producers

Speaking to a large group of top executives at a convention, Michael Jordan was quoted as saying:

"Many of you here believe that I have enjoyed a superstar career and that I am, arguably, one of the best basketball players

For a FREE 7-day course on "7 Steps To Building A Successful Marketing Plan," send an e-mail to ChipTips@ChipCummings.com

25

to ever play the game. But you forget that while I have some natural ability, it took many years and thousands of hours to develop it to the point it is today. It took years of studying the moves and routines of other great superstars, and it took a great coach like Phil Jackson to nurture, push and focus my efforts for them to become habit, and lead me to where I am today."

Before you begin your journey to join the "Michael Jordan's" of the sales world, you need to understand and study the habits of other top sales producers to learn how they gained and maintain their success. Over the years, I've worked and spoken to thousands of salespeople around the world. I have interviewed, studied and witnessed the methods, techniques, styles and habits of some of the most successful sales producers in various industries. And no matter how you slice it, there's always a common denominator.

It's not about you!

I titled this book *Stop Selling and Start Listening* for a very powerful reason. If you want to be a top producer, you have to *stop selling*! You need to realize that people *do* want to buy things, but they *don't* want to be sold anything. Top producers know this. They understand that it's not about the products or services, but rather the customer and their needs. Yes, your products have to be good, but what they are really buying is YOU! A critical part of the buying process is building a relationship of trust to reinforce their decision to buy from you. They need to rely not just on the end product, but your ability to deliver it in a way that makes it a comfortable experience. *Top Producers know that they don't sell products or services – they provide solutions and experiences!*

Top Producers train themselves to become astute listeners, and learn to recognize the customer's problem first, *before* they offer a solution. Here are several important "rules of the road" for Top Producers:

For a FREE 7-day course on "7 Steps To Building A Successful Marketing Plan," send an e-mail to ChipTips@ChipCummings.com

26

Offer outrageous customer service

Top producers do what unsuccessful sales people won't do: they go beyond what is expected of them by providing "outrageous" customer service. They become "remarkable" and create a memorable experience by doing things outside the "norm." This can take the form of a simple gift or "beyond-the-call" assistance while delivering a service. For example, I know a mortgage professional who sends a limousine to pick up his clients to take them to a closing. A Bed & Breakfast that keeps track of repeat guests' favorite newspapers, food, and music – or an insurance agent that simply calls periodically to check for coverage changes. As the CEO of Evergreen Mortgage, we created a "WOW" experience where we would present the customer with a miniature, live evergreen tree at each mortgage closing. After we started doing this we were the talk of the town! Become memorable.

Adopt a team approach

Top sales producers improve their productivity and extend their reach by using a team approach. They know what the highest and best use of their time is, and hire or delegate other activities to others who are better at those activities. Don't try to work on "weak spots", but rather concentrate on your strengths. For example, I may initiate a loan, but I have a loan processor to handle the paperwork, and we complete the transaction by using a Closing Specialist. It would not make sense for me to attempt to handle every single detail that needs to be done during the process. Make sure that every person on the team knows their position and responsibilities!

Rather than keeping their team in the dark, Top Producers make sure that their team knows every step of what goes into a successful customer transaction. They carefully document and map out the process, including key procedures and contingency plans, making sure that everyone on the team understands the organizational system flow, and the key part they play in the success of the system.

For a FREE 7-day course on "7 Steps To Building A Successful Marketing Plan," send an e-mail to ChipTips@ChipCummings.com

27

Measure Your Success

Top Producers measure their success by continuously testing and tracking their results. I have known many top money makers who acknowledge that at any moment, they have a minimum of five to seven advertisements and lead generators running in different mediums. When a lead is generated, they know exactly where it came from, so they can measure which ads and sources are paying off — and which ones are duds. If you don't measure the success of your marketing efforts, how do you know the results?

Develop trust and credibility

Your customers will only do business with you if you can deliver two things: trust and credibility. Top Producers know you can't have one without the other. If people trust you, but you don't have any credibility (or vice versa), they're not going to do business with you. Mike Baker, CEO of TheLoanOfficerStore.com cleverly puts it this way — "if you can remember *The Andy Griffith Show* from years ago, the character Barney Fife was very trustworthy, but he lacked a certain amount of credibility. On the other hand, Andy exuded a certain confidence that led us to believe we could trust him and no one doubted his credibility!"

While this can take time (sometimes minutes and at other times years), this is key to developing Evangelists, because they will perpetuate the "marketing map" cycle for you, as long as your trust and credibility remain intact.

Embrace frustration because it breeds success

I saw a sign in an office recently, that simply stated "Frustration = Success." Top Producers are restless and resolute. They aren't content to just complain about a situation, but rather programmed to do something about it. They know that complacency is the

For a FREE 7-day course on "7 Steps To Building A Successful Marketing Plan," send an e-mail to ChipTips@ChipCummings.com

28

enemy of success, and that frustration leads to developing solutions and increased productivity. The average salesperson gets frustrated with systems, procedures, products, prices, or the market — and just complains. They are always looking for "who or what" to blame their frustration on, instead of creatively finding new ideas to better the organization, process, or environment. Frustration is good.

Engage in constant learning

How much do you think you spend on haircuts over the course of a year? Is it possible that you're spending more on the outside of your head than on the inside? Some people are willing to spend anywhere from $300 to $1,500 per year on hair styling, but balk at spending $200 on a marketing seminar.

Learn your business — inside and out. Top producers continue to invest in themselves through books, college courses, degreed programs, seminars, boot camps, and personal coaching. They are constantly learning about their industry, customers, competitors, and vendors. Tiger Woods, Ernie Els and Phil Mickelson are three of the best golfers in the world, but they still seek help and guidance from coaches, and educate and train themselves to be better players tomorrow. Don't forget to invest money and resources on the inside of your head. The best way to become a Top Producer, is to learn from other Top Producers. Learn what they know, and develop the habits they have.

Present solutions in a non-threatening environment

Top Producers know that they can't talk down to customers, and must understand the "psychology of place." They know how to create a comfortable environment that encourages customer questions and develop interaction which spurs open and honest dialog (relationship building!).

For a FREE 7-day course on "7 Steps To Building A Successful Marketing Plan," send an e-mail to ChipTips@ChipCummings.com

29

For example, a friend of mine in the commercial real estate industry was working on financing a very large project in Arizona with a ranch owner. He was competing with several big banks, but he surmised that the ranch owner would feel more comfortable talking with him on his own ranch than in a bank building with a bunch of "suits." So, he dressed in jeans and a shirt, rented an old beat-up pickup truck, filled it with ice and beer, and visited the owner at his ranch. After spending time with the owner and ranch hands, he got the business and the ranch owner made a point of saying how "comfortable" it was to do business with him. Meet the customer on "their" terms — not yours. They need to feel comfortable in the process, or it will distract from the experience.

Let the CUSTOMER make the decision

Top Producers may evaluate many options for a customer, but they always reduce these down to the best two or three choices and then let the customer decide for themselves. Don't overwhelm them. Too many options will create confusion for the Prospect, and only lead them to require more time to evaluate all the options.

While I may evaluate or possess dozens of possible solutions for the Prospect, I always narrow my solutions down to two, or no more than three preferred choices. Top Producers key into the *listening process* from the beginning. They explain that their expertise enables them to present the most beneficial solutions. Then they say, "Here is why you should consider these two possibilities." At this point, as the Top Producer lays out the facts, the "closing" process is a mere formality: "Which option do you think works better for you folks today?"

There is an added advantage to this technique. Notice it isn't easy to say "No!" If I refine their options to the best single one, as in, "Here is what I think you should do... Shall we go ahead?"

For a FREE 7-day course on "7 Steps To Building A Successful Marketing Plan," send an e-mail to ChipTips@ChipCummings.com

30

the most likely answer will be "No, we want to think about it." When you provide only one choice, people are afraid they will make a mistake because they think there may be something better available. Likewise, if they describe their ideal solution, but then you offer only what's best for you (perhaps because you earn a higher commission), they will loose trust and have doubts about everything else you tell them.

With two or three choices, they are actively involved in the decision process and they feel more in control. Make them understand that you considered and evaluated many different possibilities, but your professional experience dictated that these are the best choices. Stay away from asking questions that result in simple "Yes or No" answers. Instead, ask specific choice questions such as "would Tuesday or Wednesday be better?"

The other advantage to this technique is that it reinforces the basic premise that the customer usually knows what they want better than you do. For example, I had a client that needed financing very quickly for a $48 million dollar project in the State of Washington. Based on the fast timing required in that situation, I could only offer him financing with very high interest rates and less-than-optimal terms. If I had assumed he only wanted a low interest rate, the deal could have died right there. However, after carefully asking questions and listening to him, I realized that he was happy to pay high interest for a short time because, by executing a loan within a certain time frame, he was going to save four million dollars on the payoff of the loan. Don't make the decision FOR them.

Effectively get your message in front of a moving target

Top Producers know how to effectively get their message in front of moving targets. They realize that they have to offer the right product, at the right price, to the right market, at the right

For a FREE 7-day course on "7 Steps To Building A Successful Marketing Plan," send an e-mail to ChipTips@ChipCummings.com

31

time. You may have the best product or service and sales message in the world, but if you don't put it in the right place, it doesn't matter. You wouldn't put a billboard up in the middle of the dessert, right?

In later chapters, we will look at the process of "laser-targeting" your market, by going directly where they can be found, and making sure the message of your solution matches their interpretation of their problem.

Soft sell the customer, then up-sell the benefits

You don't ask to get married on the first date, so why should you assume Prospects will buy from you the very first time they encounter you?! Top Producers know that when prospective customers come to them, they want information first. Remember, they want to find out three basic things: who you are, what you have, and why they should care, so the decision itself HAS to come second. However, many salespeople are trained to only think in terms of "close, close, close." Instead, you need to learn to "soft sell" the customer on your solution to their problem, then "up-sell" the Personal Value benefits that they get for choosing your solution. Do this by asking questions, listening, then recognizing and respecting their situation verbally.

For example, I've got a friend named Joe. When his second baby was born, he realized that the family compact car was going to be too small. He went to a car dealer and told the salesman they were looking for a $15,000 station wagon. The salesman immediately walked them across the lot and showed them a $45,000 Volvo sedan. The salesman's justification was that the luxury car was much safer. Joe and his wife understood the logic but it wasn't in their price range. Instead of indicating that he had a solution that matched their perceived problem, the salesman never GOT to sell the benefits

For a FREE 7-day course on "7 Steps To Building A Successful Marketing Plan," send an e-mail to ChipTips@ChipCummings.com

32

of his expertise. Of course, Joe left the lot without buying a car from that dealer. Because the salesman used a hard-sell strategy instead of listening, he earned 100% of nothing versus 100% of a smaller sale.

By asking more questions and using proper listening techniques, the salesman could have used a soft-sell approach which directly matched the customer's perceived need, but then up-sold the safety benefits of the more expensive vehicle. The customer would still have understood the logic, possibly agreed and purchased the luxury vehicle, but would not have felt alienated by the sales tactic. After appreciating the salesman's concerns, they could "fall back" on the more reasonably priced item, and the salesman would have gotten more than just a sale — he would have created trust and reliability (which of course is hard to do in the world of car sales!) This would earn Joe future sales, and the opportunity to create another Evangelist. Address and match the need first, then offer other solutions based upon your expertise.

Be creative and tenacious

Think outside the box. Top Producers use their creativity to connect with the right customers and realize that it takes more than one encounter to make a sale.

What if I told you I would give you a million dollars if you could arrange a meeting directly with Bill Gates, the founder of Microsoft? How would you do it? Hint: e-mail won't cut it! According to Microsoft, Bill Gates receives over four million e-mail messages PER DAY! But any Top Producer would jump at this challenge. They would develop a detailed and creative strategy for getting to Bill Gates. For example, they might use a "six degrees of separation" method in which they would ask people they knew and people who might be in a position to

For a FREE 7-day course on "7 Steps To Building A Successful Marketing Plan," send an e-mail to ChipTips@ChipCummings.com

33

know, continuing until they got closer to the one person who could introduce them to Bill Gates.

Having accomplished this, they also know that Bill will probably not buy from them the first time they talk. They know studies show that, on average, it takes six to seven contacts before someone will consider buying from them. So, having established the first connection with Bill, they won't ask for his business right away. Instead, they will seek to develop a relationship through follow-up encounters via telephone, personal meetings, affiliated decision-makers, or regular mail just to name a few.

On the flip-side, what would you do if out of nowhere, Bill Gates walked into the room? Top Producers are not only creative and tenacious, but also prepared. If you were to have the opportunity to sit down with Bill Gates, or Malcolm Forbes, or Warren Buffet for an hour, how would you spend the time? What would you say? Top Producers already know.

Chip's Seven Rules for Success

So here we are. In looking at these various traits, after working with and studying the habits of thousands of successful producers, and analyzing their habits and methods of success, I've boiled their formula down to something I call "Chip's Seven Rules for Success." On any trip, including our "Million Dollar Journey", it helps if you have certain guideposts along the way. So, here are the seven rules are in order, starting with those tasks you need to concentrate on first, as if you are starting from ground zero. I will cover some of these rules in more detail elsewhere in this book. Other rules could easily fill an entire separate book on the subject, so I will only touch on them briefly here.

For a FREE 7-day course on "7 Steps To Building A Successful Marketing Plan," send an e-mail to ChipTips@ChipCummings.com

34

1. Rule of Reality

This is the "You Are Here" arrow for your business. When you're starting a journey, you need to know where you are first, before you can begin to map where it is you want to go. This rule establishes where you are NOW. Top Producers can clearly define themselves and what they do before they start their journey.

To truly get a fix on your current location, you'll need to ask yourself these questions:

✦ What is your Unique Value Proposition (UVP)?

✦ Can you clearly define your "Personal Value" in seven seconds?

✦ Who is your direct target audience or "perfect" customer?

✦ What is your business plan to reach that target audience?

✦ What marketing and sales systems will you use?

In Chapter 4, we will look at the "Rule of Reality" in much more depth, and we will explain the process of creating your market identity.

For a FREE 7-day course on "7 Steps To Building A Successful Marketing Plan," send an e-mail to ChipTips@ChipCummings.com

35

2. Rule of Reach

Once you determine where you are and have identified your goals, your next task is to establish the rules of the road and set up a system for reaching customers. Discussed in-depth in Chapter 5, this Rule will take us through three "Rs." Research, React, and Respect.

You will start by thoroughly researching exactly what it is your target market "Prospects" want. You will quickly learn that you cannot serve everyone, so you must segment the market and decide where you will concentrate your main efforts. Who are the customers you will serve? What is their niche? Where exactly do we find them?

Then you need to react to your research. You will discover ways to analyze and target the Suspects, and develop appropriate solutions to reach them. All of your internal systems and marketing strategies need to revolve around establishing a "relational" rather than a "transactional" customer experience. Your goal is to establish a "business friendship", and position yourself as a trustworthy and reliable expert resource which satisfies their need for information — someone who exhibits a desire for future, repeat business through concern for *their* interests.

Finally, you will learn to "respect" your customers by not *selling* to them, but rather *listening* to them. You will need to establish a system where you will regularly contact Prospects six or seven times without applying the "hard sell." Through database tacking systems, you'll need to organize your customers into three types: past (customers who may purchase with you again), present (customers you are actively servicing now), and future (new customers with which you are trying to connect). Rather than focusing on just your services and

For a FREE 7-day course on "7 Steps To Building A Successful Marketing Plan," send an e-mail to ChipTips@ChipCummings.com

36

products, you'll decide what experience you want all your customers to have when they come in contact with you. Once you have mastered The Rule of Reach, you'll start filling your pipeline with laser-targeted, qualified Prospects.

3. Rule of Restlessness

Top Producers don't rest. Everyone only has 24 hours in a day, but Top Producers have figured out how to work smarter, not harder. To increase their impact, they leverage technology and spend a lot of time fine tuning their systems. They are never 100% satisfied with their marketing systems, and are constantly looking for ways to make them more effective. Complacency is not in their vocabulary, and they have an insatiable appetite for learning new ways to sharpen their skills. Remember, a sharp axe will cut down a tree in less time than a dull one, and if I only have 20 hours to cut it down, I'll spend 17 of those hours sharpening my axe. Spend more time sharpening your own axe. Constantly re-evaluate your processes, test different systems and track the results to make sure your operation is running at peak efficiency, and never become satisfied with the status quo.

Top performing salespeople also recognize that the path to success doesn't come by accident — it comes through education. They know firsthand that education can only be obtained in one of two ways: either through making mistakes or by tapping into resources that illustrate the experiences of others to avoid mistakes. Invest in the best resources you can find, including educational materials and professional coaching. Every Top Producer has someone who can identify their strengths and weaknesses, and keeps them focused on driving down the right road. Always be researching ways to avoid mistakes — it's much cheaper.

For a FREE 7-day course on "7 Steps To Building A Successful Marketing Plan," send an e-mail to ChipTips@ChipCummings.com

37

4. Rule of Retention

Top Producers know how to provide a first-class experience for their customers. They consistently under-promise and over-deliver. Mastery of this Rule will make you stand out from most salespeople who do just the opposite — the ones who over-promise and under-deliver! Not that they *try* to, but they end up promising the world just to get the sale, and then have to work twice as hard to live up to the expectation. If you promise eight things and only deliver seven, the customer will remember the one thing you missed! On the other hand, if you promise eight things and deliver ten, statistics show that they're going to tell an average of eight people about the "over-the-top" service you provided and what an enjoyable experience it was. If you fall short, they'll tell 20.

Go the extra mile to create the "WOW" effect for your customers, and turn them into Evangelists. For example, I had a client that was short one document for his real estate closing. I could have just said, "OK, just mail it and we'll delay the closing for another day or two," but I told him not to worry, I would take care of it. So, I drove one hour out of my way just to get the last document we needed to finish the closing. The customer was amazed and called to tell me that "no one else he knew would do that for him." Within the next six months, he referred five other customers to us.

5. Rule of Referrals

For Top Producers, referrals are the life-blood of future success. You do not have enough time, money, energy or resources to invest in the creation of a new customer every time you need to generate income. You will either go broke or become a victim of "burn-out."

For a FREE 7-day course on "7 Steps To Building A Successful Marketing Plan," send an e-mail to ChipTips@ChipCummings.com

38

Research shows that, for every dollar you spend retaining an existing customer, you'll spend eleven dollars trying to get a new one. Top Producers have systems for maintaining contact with their customers on a regular basis and creating an environment that encourages referrals. Known as DRIP marketing systems, these database and customer relationship management programs automate the process of relation-building. One of the best companies I have found to work with for this process is The Turning Point (www.TurningPoint.com).

Don't wait until after the sale to ask for referrals. The process starts at the very beginning of the relationship. Set the stage right at the start by indicating that you primarily work from a referral base, because you enjoy working with friends and associates of happy customers. I was recently asked by a reporter how much of my business was from referrals, and I indicated that it was over 95%. He was shell-shocked! "How can that be?" he asked.

First, I've been doing this for many years, and have built up a pretty good bank of clients. But more than that, I have a system. I have a system that has been fine-tuned so well that it works automatically — with or without me. I explained how I have reached the point in my professional career where I really get to "pick and choose" who I work with, and that I do it for the love of it — not the money. He understood the power of this completely different approach.

I have a detailed training program called "Creating The Ideal Customer" which looks at how to develop and implement a dynamic referral system. Soon to be released in an upcoming book, this process provides the blueprint for creating an automatic, repeatable yet simple system for maintaining customers, and capitalizing on the "lifetime value of the client."

Another way to keep referrals coming in for the newer salesperson is by simply keeping in touch with your

For a FREE 7-day course on "7 Steps To Building A Successful Marketing Plan," send an e-mail to ChipTips@ChipCummings.com

39

customers! A 2002 study of customers who had gone through a mortgage loan process revealed that 90% of the customers contacted could not remember after one year who their loan officer was! Other similar studies show that an average of 82% of customers cannot remember the providers of similar professional services. They might remember the company, but usually not the individual. Don't let this happen to you! You need to "touch" a customer at least four to six times a year just to remind them who you are. How do you do this? Some examples include phone calls, e-mails, free reports, article clippings, e-zines, direct mail information pieces, holiday cards, tele-conferences, or using an automated DRIP system like The Turning Point — just to name a few!

6. Rule of Relationships

Top Producers know how to nurture both internal and external relationships, and take care of key people in critical areas of support. Internal relationships include your team of employees, assistants, business and internal systems partners. There is an enormous value in creating a close-knit internal support community that you can trust and depend on, and it goes way beyond what money can buy. Treat these support people like gold. Make sure that everyone in the support system, from your top salesperson right down to your receptionist, knows your dreams, goals and business plan. When everyone is "in sync" working towards the same end, the results come faster, problems get solved quicker, and the bonds become almost unbreakable. Simple things matter, and may take the form of occasional pizza parties or casual Fridays. However you do it, make sure the people you work with understand that they are an important piece of the success puzzle, and that you take the time to share your organization's success with them.

For a FREE 7-day course on "7 Steps To Building A Successful Marketing Plan," send an e-mail to ChipTips@ChipCummings.com

40

While this type of internal community is vital for success, it is also relatively rare. Those of you who have witnessed this know what I mean, and understand the magic effect this can have in an organization. Top Producers know this as well, and strive to put the right players in key spots, and take very good care of them in many ways.

External relationships include customers and affiliate partners. I've already touched on how to take care of customer relationships in Rules four and five. Affiliate partners include anyone who supports the customer transaction outside of your organization. This can include vendors, retailers, wholesalers, and professionals providing complementary services which benefit YOUR client base. For example, in the mortgage industry there are real estate agents, builders, title companies, appraisers, certified financial planners, CPAs, and tax attorneys.

Make sure you seek out well qualified, top-notch professionals, and establish a win-win relationship with these parties. One way you can do this is to embark on some "fusion marketing" with some key players. For example, in the mortgage industry, I might target first-time home buyers as my primary customer market. Who do I know that deals directly with first-time home buyers? Real estate agents. So, I will approach real estate agents who deal with homes in the market range of a typical first-time home buyer in a particular area. NOT ones that sell multi-million dollar homes or work primarily on "listings", but rather within specific neighborhoods and price ranges.

I could just call them and say "Do you have anyone who needs to be pre-qualified for a loan?" But, then, what's in it for them? Look at them similar to the way we look at our other potential clients — determine what Personal Value you can bring to them and THEIR business. The better approach is to say "I've got some marketing ideas for you to get some new clients which

For a FREE 7-day course on "7 Steps To Building A Successful Marketing Plan," send an e-mail to ChipTips@ChipCummings.com

41

can help both of us." So, I'll propose that we co-market to first-time home buyers, and share systems and resources for greater effect. How can we do this? Just for starters, we can co-host a first-time homebuyer seminar or teleconference call. We can offer free credit reports coupled with a consultation where I go over the report with the homebuyer. We can coordinate a budgeting session with a CPA to help them understand the home budgeting process, or provide a free one-hour consultation with an interior designer to help them with decorating ideas. Then, we can market these ideas to and through first-time homebuyers by using coordinated online and physical systems.

Top Producers know that the key to these external relationships is to approach them the same as they would their other customer relationships. Find out what your external agents need. Listen to their marketing ideas and business goals, and service them as you would a customer. This will build a relationship that will pay ongoing dividends for both you and your external partners.

7. Rule of Risk

Les Brown has a quote that is a favorite of mine: "Jump first, and grow your wings on the way down!" If Gutenberg didn't take a chance on the printing press you might be reading this book as a manuscript hand-written by a monk! Another key trait of Top Producers is that they are not afraid to take calculated risks. They experiment with new strategies, particularly in technology, and are not afraid to take that leap of faith.

Studies show that there tend to be two types of people when it comes to making decisions. The first group evaluates information quickly, and acts decisively making a quick decision. This group is very slow to change their minds. The other group is just the opposite, taking a long time to make a

For a FREE 7-day course on "7 Steps To Building A Successful Marketing Plan," send an e-mail to ChipTips@ChipCummings.com

42

decision, then after receiving information are quick to change their minds. Top Producers fall into the first group. While they will not blindly make uninformed decisions, they understand the Rule of Risk, and are often willing to take a chance with a piece of technology a year or more before everyone else starts using it. Don't make rash decisions, but don't sit there and wait to see what "everyone else does" first. Embrace change and seek out cutting edge technologies that you think will give you a leg up on the competition. Then learn how to use these technologies creatively to enhance the customer experience and make your operation more effective.

Now that we know the players in the game a little better, let's get back to developing our roadmap. In the next Chapter, The Rule of Reality, we will establish where you are NOW, and develop your own UVP.

For a FREE 7-day course on "7 Steps To Building A Successful Marketing Plan," send an e-mail to ChipTips@ChipCummings.com

43

CHIP TIPS:

Here are your "personal road signs" from this Chapter:

1. It's Not About YOU!

2. Top Producers develop their relationships through Trust and Credibility.

3. Let the CUSTOMER make the decision — you need to narrow the focus of possible solutions.

4. Learn the 7 Rules of Success.

5. Top Producers know how to work smarter — not harder, and aren't afraid to take calculated risks.

For a FREE 7-day course on "7 Steps To Building A Successful Marketing Plan," send an e-mail to ChipTips@ChipCummings.com

44

Chapter 4

—

The Rule of Reality

"It is more important to know where you are going than to get there quickly. Do not mistake activity for achievement."

Mabel Newcomer

If you're starting a journey, you first need to know where you are before you can get where you want to go. Many people establish goals or objectives, but find it difficult to get there because they don't know where to start! In fact, the average salesperson never takes the time to figure out exactly what it is they are marketing to their customers. In contrast, top sales performers clearly define themselves and what they do before they start their journey.

Let's use hunting as an example. If you had to hunt to feed your village, you would first decide what game you're hunting, and then select the best tool. You can hunt a lot of smaller game or a few larger targets. Let's say you have a choice between using a rifle or a shotgun. It might take thirty or forty shotgun shells to provide the same amount of food from smaller game that you can get from one elk. So, you decide to go after the elk. However, you would never use a shotgun to bring down an elk because it doesn't have the range or accuracy. Similarly, with marketing, you can send out a lot of little projectiles in hopes of hitting something or you can use a single, focused, concentrated force which will bring down the big targets. You must develop a focused, concentrated strategy for reaching our target market.

For a FREE 7-day course on "7 Steps To Building A Successful Marketing Plan," send an e-mail to ChipTips@ChipCummings.com

45

Creating your UVP

I call this first step the *Rule of Reality*, and its main purpose is to help you develop a *UVP* or Unique Value Proposition. You may be familiar with the term "USP" or "Unique Selling Proposition", but I want to get you *away* from selling, and think about the *value* that you are bringing to the customer relationship. This rule simply means that, anyone should be able to clearly define the value and benefits that they bring to the customer within their respective industry. I learned the Rule of Reality from a friend who is a marketing master. He is very successful and has developed several infomercials and other marketing strategies that I'm sure you've seen over the years. He learned early on that you should develop your UVP in the following way:

✦ Define your industry.

✦ Recognize what specialty within that industry you are targeting.

✦ Ask yourself "What value do I bring to the marketplace that is unique?"

The process forces you to focus on something unique to you. What is so rare about you that a potential client can't easily find with someone else in your marketplace? If you were your competition, how would you define you? Develop a couple of statements that can sum that up.

Learn from Federal Express. Technically, they are in the delivery business, but there are a lot of companies in the delivery industry, so that's not what sets them apart. What's their specialty? Overnight delivery. They have a powerful UVP: "FedEx — If it positively, absolutely has to be there overnight." The consistent repetition of that phrase has made it a part of our cultural mind. Their *value* lies in the fact that they are a reliable

For a FREE 7-day course on "7 Steps To Building A Successful Marketing Plan," send an e-mail to ChipTips@ChipCummings.com

46

resource for consumers, and the benefit is "peace of mind", not to mention time-critical service! If you had an emergency and absolutely had to insure that a replacement part was going to be delivered overnight, who is the first company that comes to mind? Right. If I've got a package that has to be in Europe by tomorrow morning, there's only one place I'm going to call. However, if I'm shipping a package to California and it can wait two or three days, I'll use UPS ground service. Are there other companies that can provide the same service? Of course, but FedEx carries the torch!

What about your niche? Ask yourself, "What part of my industry am I actually in?" Narrow it down to the customers you are going to target. This makes it easier to find them. If it is a strong enough niche, revolve the whole operation around it — including the name. When you hear names like "Toys R Us" or "Babies R Us", do you have any question about their target market?

Let's take another cultural corporate example — Coca-Cola. Everybody in the world knows what industry Coca-Cola is in, but what about their value statement? There are many soft-drinks and refreshment products on the market, so how do they distinguish themselves in such a highly competitive field? Well, a brand name and multi-million dollar advertising budget doesn't hurt, but ads alone won't do it. If they didn't have a quality product, and developed a "trust relationship" with their target market, then all the advertising in the world wouldn't help in the long-run. They do it through shear numbers and establishing value within various niche markets.

Founded in 1886, Coca-Cola is the world's leading manufacturer, marketer, and distributor of non-alcoholic beverage concentrates and syrups used to produce nearly 400 beverage brands. 400 different brands! That's niche marketing. They have established various specific products designed and

For a FREE 7-day course on "7 Steps To Building A Successful Marketing Plan," send an e-mail to ChipTips@ChipCummings.com

47

marketed to produce benefits for laser-targeted audiences when it comes time for them to think of refreshments.

In my industry, I can do jumbo mortgages, construction loans and a lot of other financing, but where is my target? One of my niches is first time home buyers. I get referrals and other business from that, but I focus on my target niche first. Concentrate on your primary niche first, and then branch out.

One way you can branch out is by focusing several people within your organization on different niches. This way, each person can market to their special group. For example, when somebody calls my partner to do financing on a church property, he explains, "You know what? I do commercial financing for apartments, shopping, and office buildings. It would be better if I refer you to an associate that specializes in churches. Let me call you back in a few minutes once I've had a chance to confer with him in order to make sure that we can provide you the best possible information." This way we earn the customer's trust and respect because we provided the right resource at the right time.

To develop you own personal "UVP", start by identifying exactly what industry you are in. In my case, my primary industry is the "money business." Then examine your specialty within that industry. Again, in my case it is "residential home financing." I may also provide commercial financing and some other services, but my primary specialty is residential home financing. Other specialties within that industry include financing for boats, automobiles, checking or savings accounts, personal lines of credit, student loans, etc.

Finally, take a close look at the niche market you serve within that specialty. This is the step that the average salesperson doesn't get around to, but Top Producers do! It's not enough to say "I serve anybody that needs financing." That may be the case, but that isn't what Prospects want to hear! They want

For a FREE 7-day course on "7 Steps To Building A Successful Marketing Plan," send an e-mail to ChipTips@ChipCummings.com

48

For a FREE 7-day course on "7 Steps To Building A Successful Marketing Plan," send an e-mail to ChipTips@ChipCummings.com

49

someone they consider an expert and that they can trust. Niche markets that I attack are first-time homebuyers and the self-employed borrower. In fact, I go further, and establish sub-niches such as self-employed medical professionals and attorneys! Is a loan application for a self-employed doctor handled any differently than a plumber or a freelance artist? No, of course not, but THEY think there is a difference! By specializing in the marketplace, I am seen as a qualified expert who understands their individual needs, which will bring in more direct referrals.

Here's another example. Say you were preparing to build an addition onto your home. You call a carpenter in to discuss the project, and he indicates that he can handle the "rough-in" and finish carpentry work. You ask about a referral for an electrician, roofer, plumber, painter, etc. only to have the carpenter reply that he can do all those jobs! Sounds great, right — one stop shopping. Not exactly. By professing that he can personally handle all those jobs, he has just watered down his carpentry skills, and lost a lot of credibility. Jack of all trades is a master of none, remember? Set yourself apart by creating a UVP that centers around the benefit and value that you bring to your target market.

Developing Your Seven-Second Pitch

After you create your UVP, you need to narrow it down and develop a "seven-second statement" that clearly and concisely identifies your value to the Prospect. This is key for developing your marketing strategy, since if you can't quickly and clearly describe what you do, how will the customer ever know what the benefit or value is for them in doing business with you?

The seven-second statement must be positioned as a benefit statement for the Prospect, NOT a statement about what business you're in! There is a BIG difference. Your must

For a FREE 7-day course on "7 Steps To Building A Successful Marketing Plan," send an e-mail to ChipTips@ChipCummings.com

50

memorize your statement, and be prepared to explain it to anyone and everyone by habit, in any given situation. Imagine you are standing in an elevator and in walks somebody who says, "Hi, my name is John. What is it that you do?" They punch a button and you see they are only traveling one floor. You have seven-seconds to capture their attention. Do you know what you would say before that person leaves the elevator?

If I'm at a convention, the person on that elevator may be the president of IBM or a corporate executive planning to relocate 2,000 employees to my town. My statement must be clear and strong enough to make them desire to know more. For example, I could reply, "I'm in the mortgage industry" or "I write mortgages." Do you think either of these statements is powerful enough to inspire someone to ask for more information? Instead, if I shook their hand and said, "I'm Chip. I supply money for people to live the American dream," do you think their curiosity would be aroused? They might ask, "Wow, how do you do that?" If you can't concisely and accurately, tell someone what you do in that very limited time, 2,000 deals might walk right out those elevator doors and you'll never even know it.

I suggest you develop more than one seven-second pitch. Develop different ones for different situations. For example, if I'm at a casual social gathering with people from all kinds of professions, and someone asks me, "What do you do?" I've got a couple different statement options. One of my favorites is "I give away money." Through the law of "consistent predictability", I can predict their response with over 90% accuracy — "Oooo... give some to me!" or something along those lines. My standard reply is "but there's one catch — People have to pay it back." It opens the door and starts the conversation. They say, "What do you mean you give away money?" I answer, "Well, I have the pleasure of financing people's dreams by helping families buy their first home."

For a FREE 7-day course on "7 Steps To Building A Successful Marketing Plan," send an e-mail to ChipTips@ChipCummings.com

51

Much of my time now is spent speaking to organizations and sales professionals around the world. My seven-second statement for this purpose is "I specialize in teaching sales professionals and business owners how to use creative technology to attract, capture, convert and retain new customers". See how that gets the benefit point across, while opening the door for them to walk right in?

Spend some time on this exercise. It will challenge you to develop an impact driven, consumer-benefit oriented, seven-second statement. Experiment. Write it and rewrite it until it is refined and evokes a powerful picture of your benefit to your client. Then memorize it. Practice it until you are saying it in your sleep. Speak it every morning; post it to your mirror. Memorize it until it's so much a part of you that when somebody walks by and says, "Hi, I'm John; I work at UPS. What do you do?" Your words enfold them with a desire to know more. Once you develop this seven-second statement, you are ready to proceed to the next phase — The Rule of Reach!

For a FREE 7-day course on "7 Steps To Building A Successful Marketing Plan," send an e-mail to ChipTips@ChipCummings.com

52

CHIP TIPS:

Here are your "personal road signs" from this Chapter:

To get a fix on your current location, ask yourself these questions:

1. What is your Unique Value Proposition (UVP)?

2. Who is your perfect customer?

3. What are the BENEFITS that you offer the Prospects?

4. Can you explain yourself in seven seconds?

5. Does your current marketing project your Personal Value, and get the point across in seven seconds or less?

For a FREE 7-day course on "7 Steps To Building A Successful Marketing Plan," send an e-mail to ChipTips@ChipCummings.com

53

For a FREE 7-day course on "7 Steps To Building A Successful Marketing Plan," send an e-mail to ChipTips@ChipCummings.com

54

Chapter 5

The Rule of Reach

"Ability is what you're capable of doing.
Motivation determines what you do.
Attitude determines how well you do it."

Lou Holtz

Our next guidepost is the Rule of Reach, and this is the biggie! On our million dollar journey, we now know where we are, and have defined the path we want to travel. This chapter will get us started on the journey and put the foot on the gas! Here we lay out the rules of the road and set up the system we will use to reach our customers. We will define the three types of customers and understand how reaching and capturing these customers differs when we apply the Rule of the Four R's.

Three types of customers: past, present, and future

Each business has only three types of customers: past, present, and future. Depending on your target market niche and group, you will use different methods to reach each of these groups.

To make this concept a little clearer, imagine that your business is running a passenger train on a luxury railroad. Your past customers are in the passenger cars attached to the engine. If you have treated them fairly and honestly, providing an excellent transportation experience, they will continue to refer

For a FREE 7-day course on "7 Steps To Building A Successful Marketing Plan," send an e-mail to ChipTips@ChipCummings.com

55

others to your railroad. Acting as the conductor, you need to stay in contact with them, check to see that their needs are met, and remind them that you can help them with their next trip. By providing this kind of service, you strive to remain the first person they think of when they need your services again.

Present customers are riding with you in the locomotive. They are directly and actively participating with you in taking them where they want to go. Since they are new to the train, they have a lot of questions. In addition to helping them get where they want to go, you make sure they enjoy the experience so they will continue to ride your train in the passenger cars as happy past customers.

Future customers are people out there considering a ride on your train for the first time. Unfortunately, most salespeople spend too much time focusing on future customers and not enough on satisfying their existing passengers. Subconsciously you hear them say, "I'm so busy trying to get new prospects, I forgot about my past customers!"

To run a growing railroad, you have to spend the bulk of your time on past and present customers. Why? Because they send you the future ones. Will you have to spend some time reaching future customers? Of course, but you will rely heavily on technology to tackle a great portion of that. You don't ask every person individually if they want a ride on the train, you rely on schedule boards, informational signs, pamphlets, etc. to direct interested parties to the station! As you build your own railroad, you will devote some time to broad marketing efforts, but make sure you don't forget those who are already riding your train. Spend the majority of your time on the Evangelists, not the Suspects!

For a FREE 7-day course on "7 Steps To Building A Successful Marketing Plan," send an e-mail to ChipTips@ChipCummings.com

56

Transactional vs. Relational Marketing

Unfortunately, most people in business work on a transactional basis. They think, "I've got to finish with these customers quickly, so I can get back to the business of filling my system with new leads."

Business people who adopt the transactional approach often look like someone rushing through a business cycle. If I adopted this attitude in the mortgage business it would look something like this: "You need a mortgage? Great! Here's the document. Sign it, give me the money, then move into your house. You're happy now, aren't you?" Perhaps the customer is pleased with my efficiency for the moment, but I haven't developed a relationship with them, so they feel no loyalty. Hence, no basis for return business or referrals.

There is a more powerful, less stressful method (both for you and the customer!). It's called *relational* marketing. Unlike transactional thinking where business people treat clients like "a quick payday," relational marketing establishes a business friendship, provides a resource for their need for information, and suggests a desire for future, repeat business. The best way to create a relationship-based transaction is to ask questions, listen for the answers, and then ask more questions! According to a study done at UCLA in Southern California, the average 5-year old asks 65 questions per day! When you get a response, learn to ask another "deeper" question based upon the answer. This communicates that you care about the customer and their problem, and directs you to a clearer solution.

Here's an example of how I could establish a relationship by building trust:

> "You want to move into a new house. Tell me more
> about your situation so I insure that I recommend the
> products that serve you best. Oh, you've got three

For a FREE 7-day course on "7 Steps To Building A Successful Marketing Plan," send an e-mail to ChipTips@ChipCummings.com

57

kids? This is only a three-bedroom house. Are you looking at having more kids? You are! In a couple of years, you may be looking at upgrading to another property because you're going to run out of room. What we need to discuss is what mortgage would benefit your growing family best — that's not necessarily a 30 year fixed. There are other programs that better provide for your changing needs. I can explain the advantages quite clearly and briefly. Please answer a few more questions so I can select the one that's most cost effective for you. Do you anticipate changes in your job? Is your income going up dramatically? What's going to happen to your expenses? I understand you are paying for an older daughter's college education right now. Will those expenses disappear in two years?"

Do you see how this non-threatening interview convinces my potential client that their best interest is the basis of my questions? Imagine how this transaction relates to their world. I approach it as a conversation, not an interrogation. Most merchants just want a customer's money and then move on to the next client. When you adopt this relational approach, you'll stand out like a lighthouse on a dark, foggy night.

The conversation continues:

"Since there is a high likelihood you're going to move in a couple of years AND you have college tuition, you would benefit from an increased cash flow now. Even if you don't move, you'll benefit from having more money in the bank. I have products that offer you a lower rate now, and thus a lower payment. I'll explain two of these and you can pick. When I finish, ask me any questions you have."

For a FREE 7-day course on "7 Steps To Building A Successful Marketing Plan," send an e-mail to ChipTips@ChipCummings.com

58

By providing them a choice, the customer is engaged in deciding what fits them best. They feel in control of their decision-making process. By adopting a relational marketing stance, I act more as a caring and concerned teacher. I've developed a trusting relationship by listening and, hopefully, built a relationship that lasts.

The Rule of the Four R's

The next leg of our journey follows the Rule of the Four R's. The R's are *research*, *react*, *respect*, and *referrals*. These rules establish the basic system you'll use to determine your niche and reach past, present, and future customers.

Research

The first part of the rule is to do your *research*. Once you can clearly identify what problem(s) your target market suffers, the easier it will be for you to formulate your services and offer a plan. You could be the absolute best there is, but unless you learn through research where your market lives, you could be waiting for clients for a very, very long time. If you are the best, and you've done this first step, you are going to have people beating down your door.

Once you really establish yourself, your customers will come to you, even if you are remotely located. For example, a world famous Rolls Royce body specialist lived in a tiny town in Oklahoma. Due to great marketing through his reputation for quality work, Rolls owners who suffered dents would ship their cars to him by railroad. He did the repairs and then returned the automobiles to the owners via the same route. The repairman enjoyed the quality of life he desired by researching his niche and discovering that his customers would gladly suffer any cost or delay if it meant someone could return their machine to near perfection.

For a FREE 7-day course on "7 Steps To Building A Successful Marketing Plan," send an e-mail to ChipTips@ChipCummings.com

59

The same concept won't work for other industries however. I have a consulting client in the San Francisco area, where the average loan amount for their customers is around $1.3 million. I don't care HOW good you are at processing and closing FHA-insured loans, there just isn't a market for it in that area! Make sure you know that you have customers in your immediate area, or your product and/or service is so unique that they will come to you. Also research your competitors. No competition is a bad thing, as that means no Prospects in your neighborhood! Find out and analyze how your competitors are reaching the target market, and look for trends, inefficiencies, and "holes" in the marketplace of underserved prospects.

Analyze your competition

A lot of people begin a business without thinking about their competition. Competition isn't ugly and hard to get along with. Rivalry is actually a great thing. Competition not only brings more people into your marketplace, but gives you the opportunity to feed off their advertising.

Here's an example: Restaurant owner A opens a restaurant, but he doesn't think about where his customers will come from or what his competition offers. He gives no thought to research whatsoever. He puts his eatery in the middle of a cornfield with no roads, no parking lot, and no way to get there. He's not going to get a lot of customers, is he?

Restaurant owner B also decides she is going to open up a restaurant, but she opens it right downtown and across from another restaurant. Why does she do this? Well, did you ever notice that gas stations and car dealerships are often located near each other? There is a very good reason. People will not necessarily cross the street on the left side in order to get the service that they find on the right.

For a FREE 7-day course on "7 Steps To Building A Successful Marketing Plan," send an e-mail to ChipTips@ChipCummings.com

60

McDonald's found this out a long time ago. If there is a McDonald's on one side of street, in some places you drive two miles and there's one on the other side of the street! McDonalds proved through research that customers react a certain way, and it's more profitable to have multiple sites with different access – even when they're close together. Ray Kroc, then the head of McDonalds, was asked to talk about being in the hamburger business. He replied, "I'm not in the hamburger business; I'm in the real estate business." He went on to explain that the placement of his restaurants was as important as the product.

Find out who the competitors are in your niche, and what their "location" is within the industry, so you can provide better (price, quality or service) than they do. Competition is a good thing. If you have competitors, you picked a good market. If there are no competitors, you've got a major problem, as that probably means there is no market for your service. The exception would be if you are so specialized or the product is so new that rivals haven't found it yet — highly unlikely!

Sometimes, your "competition" can provide some of your best referrals. For example, if I'm working with my competitors in the mortgage industry, I might say, "My niche is first time homebuyers. Since you specialize in home equity lending programs, if I feed you customers, will you give me some leads in my specialty?" Using this concept, I've enjoyed some great joint ventures over the years. Try to find "compatible competitors" to create a synergistic relationship with.

Specialize to profitize

Exactly how do you discover your niche? I use a concept that I nicknamed "specialize to profitize." Since consumers are bombarded with so many choices, being "all things to all people" isn't appealing. So, you must learn to specialize.

For a FREE 7-day course on "7 Steps To Building A Successful Marketing Plan," send an e-mail to ChipTips@ChipCummings.com

61

When I was thirsty as a kid, the choice of beverage was simple: I bought a soft drink. Today's stores offer colas, fruit drinks, waters, flavored waters, high energy drinks, memory enhancing beverages, etc. I actually have to ask myself as I approach the cooler, "What kind of thirst am I seeking to satisfy, and is there a healthy alternative?" Ask yourself: does your consumer want a generic beverage or a specialty drink?

"Specialize to Profitize" means more than just having a focused market. It means catering to the needs and perceived desires of the target market. For example, imagine you are called into the doctor's office. You close the door and sit down. Your heart races as you listen to the words you dreaded to hear: "I'm sorry, but the tests came back positive. It's cancer, and it's spreading into your lungs..." I certainly hope you never go through that experience, but what would you do if you found yourself in these shoes? If it were me, I would definitely get a second opinion. I wouldn't start shopping for the lowest priced surgeon, pricing out cheap hospital operating rooms, or start trying to find a good deal on surgical specialists through the Internet! I would get recommendations and search out the best darn lung cancer specialist in the country, perhaps the world!

As business people, we may not deal with the same scary "life-or-death" issues but we can learn lessons from that example as consumers become smarter shoppers and the market begins to tighten. Don't target customers that price out the operating rooms and want 13 estimates before they can make a decision. One of the biggest mistakes you can make is trying to service the wrong kind of customer.

Specializing also means that you pick the customers you want to work with and suggest that the difficult ones move on. While you may regret the temporary loss of business, you will rejoice when you have more time to take new, less troublesome clients.

For a FREE 7-day course on "7 Steps To Building A Successful Marketing Plan," send an e-mail to ChipTips@ChipCummings.com

62

Many businesses will go after the "general" market, trying to capture any sale that comes their way. There will tend to be far too many "general practitioners" in any business, but the Top Producers know exactly what their niche is and how to reach it. Don't try to be like the handyman that can do it all-fix the plumbing, wire the electrical, and install the countertops, after putting in the furnace. Instead of being an "average" merchant, think about becoming a true specialist in your marketplace. Often you find higher-caliber clients who tend to seek out specialists that understand their unique needs and situations. They are far less likely to price shop you because they know you are a specialist. They want the experts and don't mind paying a fair price for specialized service. Investors and wholesalers have understood this for a long time and have developed specialty markets dedicated to one or two particular types of products.

Plan your attack

Here is a step-by-step guide for establishing yourself as the local specialist in your market:

1. **Decide what specialty you want to attack.** Look at your background and interests. Did you previously work in the insurance industry? Are you a volunteer firefighter? Tackle a market you know well and in which you enjoy working. As an example, if you were a loan officer, I would advise you look into areas like the entertainment market (sports, music, theatre, etc.), doctors, attorneys, construction lending, first-time homebuyers, or properties in a specific geographic area such as a resort. Make your chosen niche large enough so that it can support your business but small enough to clearly define.

For a FREE 7-day course on "7 Steps To Building A Successful Marketing Plan," send an e-mail to ChipTips@ChipCummings.com

63

2. **Go where they go.** Make yourself visible and accessible within that market. Join their associations, go to their meetings, read newsletters, and write articles targeted for that audience. Learn everything you can about their world. This will help you understand their needs and invite them to feel comfortable with you as an experienced specialist. Remember, people only do business with people they trust and only trust people they like. In the professional services arena, they need to feel as if you are "one of them."

3. **Market yourself in their world.** Don't just expect them to come to you. Create an on-line and off-line presence that reaches them in unique ways. In the off-line world, use small ads in specific industry newsletters, magazines, or trade publications. There are special publications for everything and anything you can think of! This is less expensive than traditional advertising and is highly targeted to your specific audience. Direct this traffic to automated response systems as explained in steps 4 through 6. I discuss additional strategies in more detail in Chapter 7 in more detail.

For online marketing, use specific searches to locate "keywords" that your target group hits regularly. Keywords are words or phrases that someone might type into a search engine to attempt to find a business like yours. One free tool you can use is Overture's (now owned by Yahoo!) search term suggestion tool (www.inventory.overture.com), or another is the "Good Keywords" tool available at www.GoodKeywords.com. Using these tools, you can enter words that match your target market and evaluate the number of Internet searches conducted on a monthly basis. This indicates where your market is spending their time on-line! You can then use the search statistics to create online ads with Google AdWords and other systems that direct your target market directly to you when they are using the Internet. You can also develop links to affiliate sites that are

For a FREE 7-day course on "7 Steps To Building A Successful Marketing Plan," send an e-mail to ChipTips@ChipCummings.com

64

regularly visited by your target market. In most cases for professional services, when customers find you online, you are not specifically trying to sell them your services on the spot, but rather to capture their name and contact information. Chapter 7 will cover several online marketing strategies in greater depth.

4. **Create informative electronic reports for your target market.** Remember, it's not about you and your products, but the information *they* want to know about. So, combine your professional experience with information appropriate for their niche. For example, in my field of mortgage lending, I might create a report on establishing a household budget or understanding credit reports designed for a first-time homebuyer.

   Include specific examples so that clients can learn valuable information, and then end the piece with examples of your credentials as a specialist. For example, if I targeted a highly specialized group, like doctors, I might develop a report which includes published articles or statistics on effectively managing a growing medical practice. Then I would end the report by including examples of how I assisted self-employed medical professionals finance their new home. Chapter 7 will also look at methods for creating Personal Value, including these types of reports.

5. **Keep in touch with them.** Create automated e-mail systems (autoresponders) so you can include personalized information and keep your target customers abreast of specific industry developments. Remember, change is occurring all the time, so regularly contact them with new information. Don't make it a hardcore sales pitch. Instead, position yourself to be in the right place at the right time with the right solution when they are ready to buy. You don't know if that will be two months or two years from now, but you'll never know if you give up on

For a FREE 7-day course on "7 Steps To Building A Successful Marketing Plan," send an e-mail to ChipTips@ChipCummings.com

65

them just before they are ready to make a move. This concept will be covered in more detail in Chapter 8.

6. **Create an e-zine that reflects your specialized knowledge within your target group.** An *e-zine* is an electronic newsletter that provides timely and specific information to your niche market. People like to get quick, relevant news specific to their interests or profession. Keep it to one or two pages, maximum. If you make your electronic "magazine" quick and to the point, without selling, people will remain subscribed. If they receive good, usable content, people won't mind seeing a promotion for your business every once in awhile. Chapter 9 will take a close look at developing and distributing e-zines.

7. **Service your target group with affiliated services and products.** Make product recommendations with joint-venture partners. This not only opens the door to new referrals from other professionals within your respective target groups, but enhances your professional credibility as a well-rounded specialist.

8. **Under-promise and over-deliver.** While this sounds simple and basic, this is where the average business person falls short. Far too many sales professionals promise their clients the world and merely fulfill the basics of an order, or worse, entirely disappoint the customer. If, for example, you know you can deliver an item the next day, suggest that you can have it there in three days. When it arrives the next day, the customer is very impressed.

   Develop a solid **written** plan within your operation of **exactly** how you will deliver the customer experience. Don't leave out any details. Make sure every member of your team reads it, understands it, supports it, and breathes it! If not, all your efforts will be in vain. Remember, word will spread fast within your specialized market, both positively and negatively.

For a FREE 7-day course on "7 Steps To Building A Successful Marketing Plan," send an e-mail to ChipTips@ChipCummings.com

66

React

The second of the four R's is to *react*. Now that you have a market and you've focused your aim on a target within it, you need to analyze your suspects, develop solutions to reach them, turn them into prospects, then into loyal friends.

When I say "Analyze suspects" I mean figuring out exactly who you do and do not want to work with. For example, there are a lot of realtors in my town that are very good. There are a lot of agents that sell homes to first time homebuyers. However, there are probably only about 30 percent of them with whom I want to work, and several that I don't! After a few years in this industry, I figured out that I get to pick and choose who I want to work with.

Once, as a loan officer calling on a certain real estate office, there were several agents I didn't want to give the time of day because they were rude, unreasonable people. There were others that nobody else wanted to work with. Due to my direct approach, I seemed to click with this second group, so I focused on developing solutions for this crowd. They quickly moved from prospects to loyal friends.

I reacted to my market and adjusted. I avoided people I didn't want to work with, identified the people I did want to work with, developed solutions for this group, and moved them from prospects to friends.

Respect

The third part of the Rule of the Four R's is *Respect*. This is also a key area where most salespeople go wrong. You need to respect the research that you've done and the needs of the target market. Too often, salespeople think they are smarter than the customer, so they ignore the research and do what they want anyway — only to be doomed to mediocrity! To succeed with respect you

For a FREE 7-day course on "7 Steps To Building A Successful Marketing Plan," send an e-mail to ChipTips@ChipCummings.com

67

must stop selling, ask questions, accept that you will need to make six to seven customer contacts before they buy from you, and respect the experience that the Prospect has to go through.

Stop selling!

The moment you try to sell something to someone is the moment you lose. People don't want to be sold; they want to buy on their terms. Listen to what they say and they will tell you what they want to buy, and under what conditions.

Let's pretend that I want you to buy a paperclip. "It's a nice, large clip, isn't it? I know you've got to have one of those, and it will only cost you $1.00. Do you mind writing me a check right now?" You're thinking, "What? Are you nuts?" You don't want to be sold. Instead, I should listen to what you want.

So, let's try it this way:

I say, "Wow, you seem a bit overwhelmed."

"Hey, I'm looking for a way to keep all these papers together."

I reply, "Really? Do you have a lot of papers?"

"I'm holding about 100 of them; some keep falling out of my pile all the time."

"Would it help you if I could demonstrate a way to keep large batches of papers together so they don't keep separating from their pile?"

"Show me," you plead.

"This gadget right here opens on one side. You put it on like this and it keeps all those papers together for you."

At this point, I have a solution to your problem, and you're interested. If I get you interested enough, a reasonable price certainly isn't an issue, is it? If it solves your problem, then I say,

For a FREE 7-day course on "7 Steps To Building A Successful Marketing Plan," send an e-mail to ChipTips@ChipCummings.com

68

"Great, it's going to cost you $1.00. And, the best news is they come in a box of 100 so you'll have plenty when this situation arises again." The truth is you only need one clip right now, but you'll gladly pay a dollar today even though it might be weeks before you need another. At this point, price becomes a minor point. When buyers are interested in your solution, price goes out the window.

Listen and ask MORE questions

Listen to what the customer is saying indirectly in the beginning. If the customer says "I've got these papers all over the place." Reply, "Tell me more." This is an open ended question, so they can not give you an easy "Yes" or "No" answer.

So, they answer, "The mess is causing me a lot of problems. I need to keep these papers together."

I reply, "How bad is the problem; does this happen often?" And so on.

The answers customers provide are more important than any conclusion you might jump too quickly. Do you have a long-term solution? Maybe another question or two would clarify and solidify your suggestion. Ask questions, listen carefully, and figure out if you have a solution that is in the customer's best interest. Does it really solve their problem or does it just get you a commission? Honesty and sincerity builds long term, residual clients, and builds the foundation for a good referral business.

Make six to seven customer contacts

You wouldn't get married on the first date, right? So, why do you expect your customers to buy from you the first time they encounter you? Typically, it takes six to seven contacts before someone makes a major purchase decision.

For a FREE 7-day course on "7 Steps To Building A Successful Marketing Plan," send an e-mail to ChipTips@ChipCummings.com

69

For example, it may seem that anyone could drive into McDonald's and make their decision right away without ever having heard of the company. However, chances are they have been there before. Considering that most of us grew up exposed to McDonald's advertising, it's very likely that McDonalds established plenty of customer contacts before we ever tried our first hamburger there.

If somebody walks in and says to me, "Hi, I'm thinking of buying a house." I would never dream of saying, "Oh, fantastic; you need to sign here. We've got a seven year ARM that's going to work out perfectly. You're payments are going to be this..." Whoa! Time-out! I'm completely turning them off because I'm not trying to solve their key house-buying problems.

You increase the chance a customer will buy from you when you spend the time to understand their problem. That's when you apply your listening skills. It doesn't matter whether you're in dry cleaning or food preparation. If you apply your listening skills to your market research, you can make your questions very precise. Then when customers come to your doorstep, you know they sought you out because you can offer them what they need.

Define the experience

Respect your customer's experience. It is extremely important to take a step back for a moment, and look objectively at what I call their "cradle to grave" experience-the customer's entire experience while doing business with you.

As I explained earlier, there are three phases of customer's experience: future, present, and past. Each person who utilizes your service or products passes from first time contact (potential future customer), to satisfied client (present), to repeat business (past with potential to purchase again), or a referral machine (happy past client — aka Evangelist!).

For a FREE 7-day course on "7 Steps To Building A Successful Marketing Plan," send an e-mail to ChipTips@ChipCummings.com

70

Map out the entire process. Start by asking yourself, "What is their first direct impression?" For example, how many times have you called a company and they sounded "bored" or even annoyed? Doesn't that turn off a potential customer?

Instead, what if they handled the call this way:

"Hi, this is Joe Land, ABC Mortgage. How can I help you today?"

"I'm thinking about purchasing a home."

"Fantastic! We've got specialists that help you with choosing the right financial program for your family and we guide you easily through the process. If you'll hold for just a moment, let me find an expert for you."

That's a whole different experience from simply saying "Hello" and being put on hold for five minutes. You've impressed the customer with the fact that you care, and that you'll listen to determine their best solution.

That experience should carry over from the phone to the moment they meet you or anybody else in your office. In my mortgage business, I make sure the positive experience carries through in every phase of the transaction, from the initial phone call and application to the close on their loan — and their life thereafter. My relationships with my customers don't stop when they get their money at the closing table.

Imagine the whole experience your customer goes through. Is it as satisfying for them as you can make it? If you were them, are you certain that you would do business with your company again, or recommend you to other people? If you "walk a mile in their shoes," you might see some areas of your process that you could improve. Document it. I mean every stage and every step that a customer goes through. On paper, write out the perfect customer experience from start to finish. From the moment they first come in contact with you or anyone in your office, what happens? Take a close look at the entire process, including each

For a FREE 7-day course on "7 Steps To Building A Successful Marketing Plan," send an e-mail to ChipTips@ChipCummings.com

71

person that handles each function along the way, and how the customer comes out at the end.

Once you have documented the perfect experience, then come up with at least five possible problems (or side steps) that they might encounter for each step along the way. Determine exactly what you will do for each scenario to get them BACK to the ultimate customer experience timeline. Ask past customers and your internal team to come up with the five side-steps. I'm sure they won't have any problem listing them out!

Now, you need to share this customer map with EVERY person on your team. They need to know exactly what is supposed to happen, otherwise it won't.

What NOT to do

As you can imagine, I do a lot of traveling. Recently I was traveling through a Chicago airport on my way to Atlanta, and had an experience that illustrates what happens when you do NOT properly define the customer experience.

We boarded the airplane just fine, but sat and waited until an announcement came from the pilot that there was a mechanical problem and we would have to wait for maintenance to come aboard and repair the item. After about another 45 minutes of waiting, the pilot reported that they were still working on the problem, but realizing that many people had already missed connections, instructed us that anyone who wanted to could get off the plane and rebook their schedule could do so.

Of course there was some confusion as people tried to figure out whether to leave or stay, but most stayed another 30 minutes or so, until the pilot then indicated that they would have to vacate the plane, and re-board us when the plane was ready. Upon exiting the plane, the customer service personnel were caught completely off guard. Amid their confusion, they

For a FREE 7-day course on "7 Steps To Building A Successful Marketing Plan," send an e-mail to ChipTips@ChipCummings.com

72

decided it was better to have anyone who had a flight connection in Atlanta stay the night in Chicago and fly out in the morning. Meanwhile, I noticed that there was another flight by the same airline headed to Atlanta, and leaving in 30 minutes — right at the gate next door!

It was only after they had already booked everyone's hotel, that they realized there were over 75 vacant seats on that next flight, so they decided to have any displaced passengers placed on that flight, starting with the ones who had connections (that's right, the same ones they had just sent to the hotel!) They would not allow passengers like me, who were going straight to Atlanta on the new flight until all "connection" passengers had been boarded, which of course was a problem because they had just sent them all to the hotel. The resulting holdup was now delaying the second flight. Finally, a flight attendant came out and just shouted for anyone going to Atlanta to get on the plane! We didn't even have boarding passes! Once we were actually on the flight, the resulting comments and negative attitudes that followed, by both the passengers and the flight crew, was entertaining to say the least, and made the airline look ridiculous.

To top it off, I received a letter of apology from the airline a week later, indicating that they were enclosing a gift due to the inconvenience I experienced. The gift was a $10 pre-paid long distance phone card, which expired in 60 days! The entire experience was comical, and a true example of the disaster that can result in not properly designing the customer experience and planning out the roadblocks and detours.

One of the most enlightening experiments you can do to test the experience your company is providing, is to become a "mystery caller" to your business. For example, I periodically call my own company and pretend I am a customer. Then, I access how my staff greet me and react to my needs. To get a

For a FREE 7-day course on "7 Steps To Building A Successful Marketing Plan," send an e-mail to ChipTips@ChipCummings.com

73

more objective view, I ask my friends in the industry to call and "shop me." Then, I interview them and ask questions like, "Who did you talk to? What did they say? How did you feel?" I also offer to reciprocate by acting as a mystery caller for their business. My goal is not to beat-up my staff, I just want to find out how I can make my customers feel better when they are on the phone dealing with my team.

Take the time to examine your customer experience and test it out. What you find may surprise you.

Referrals

The last "R" stands for *Referrals*, and it's a key ingredient — like icing on the cake! People love to refer other people to a great experience — its human nature. We all should be working for referrals, and Evangelists bring you referrals. Everyone knows that word of mouth is the best advertising, as it is both cheap and effective. Are you more likely to buy because you hear or saw a commercial, or because a friend raved about a product or service?

You've probably heard the profound but sometime over-simplified adage: "It's not what you know, it's who you know." A top marketing strategist I met once reformatted this statement to read "It's not who you know, it's who knows you." I think this is a more powerful truth. When your customer leaves your office, you can say you know them, but do you really? More importantly, do they leave with a feeling of confidence? Do they really know you?

Just because I know you, doesn't mean you are going to bring me referrals. The people that know and trust me are the one's who will bring me other Prospects. These are potential customers that I don't know initially, and I might never have met if previous clients and my friends didn't recommend me to them.

For a FREE 7-day course on "7 Steps To Building A Successful Marketing Plan," send an e-mail to ChipTips@ChipCummings.com

74

It's only when they really know me, and the value that I bring to the transaction, that they will then talk to their friends. You might hear a friend say to you, "There's a house down the street that went up for sale and we're thinking of purchasing it."

If you've gotten to know me and personally experienced my sincere interest in helping you with your own situation, you will probably reply "I know somebody that can help you with that. You call this guy; he's great. His name is Chip and here's his number. Tell him I referred you." That's human nature, and consistent predictability. That's also the kind of relationship I strive to build, and it's what you need to strive for with your referrals.

Earlier I used the train metaphor to describe the different types of customers. Your business is like that train. It's either moving or sitting still. It's only when it's moving that work is getting done or progress is being made. You are the engine of your business and you drive the train.

By yourself, as a solitary engine, you can only transport very few people in the locomotive part of the train. As a solitary engine, you spend a lot of your time looking for those few potential clients you alone might encounter on your journey. However, when you satisfy a client, you create a new car behind your engine. While your locomotive is moving forward, the cars behind become walking, talking invitations to future customers to enjoy your ride. The more customers, the more cars. Each additional car has the potential space to welcome more people aboard your train. Once those travelers or clients have benefited from their experience with you, they invite more people into your cars. They know they can count on your locomotive to carry their friends and family where they want to go in a pleasant environment.

Our potential clients might not know where to find a good locomotive. They might do some research (yellow pages,

For a FREE 7-day course on "7 Steps To Building A Successful Marketing Plan," send an e-mail to ChipTips@ChipCummings.com

75

commercials, friends, etc.). This may bring them to the train station, but it doesn't mean they will board your train. If they do find your engine, you're in luck. But, if your small train starts to pull out of the station right when they get there, you will be gone before they can jump on board. In addition, if you're not there, the next train that comes along will pick them up. That's your competition.

However, if you build a long train, you increase the opportunity for someone to jump on board even as your train is pulling out. If you keep creating new cars hooked to your locomotive, even though you may never see a potential passenger approaching your train, you've made yourself more visible to them through your satisfied customers. Even if you start to pull away from the platform when they walk into the station, present and past customers in one of your cars are still holding the doors open and encouraging them to jump on board. So, the more cars that follow you, the more your previous work continues to attract people you don't know. It creates a "snowball" effect that can catapult your business into what's known as "critical mass" where it takes on a life of its own!

Top Producers realize this. They don't just look at the here and now. They build that long, powerful train and say, "At some point in time you're going to need me and when you do, I'm going to be there, either directly or through an association I've developed with a satisfied customer." Your goal is to build the longest, most powerful train in your industry.

Referrals are one of the fastest ways to accelerate your business. I know it seems difficult, but it's not as tough as you might think. If you have structured the customer experience correctly, the Evangelists will be created. You just need to understand how to tap into their power. Simply enlarge your network based on referrals, and reward people for continually supporting your success.

For a FREE 7-day course on "7 Steps To Building A Successful Marketing Plan," send an e-mail to ChipTips@ChipCummings.com

76

Learn from the Domino Theory

Defining the customer experience needs to include the integrated marketing of your UVP as well. If done correctly, this is another great way to build customer referrals. I refer to this as the Domino Theory.

This theory doesn't come from tipping the Domino blocks, but rather from the Domino's Pizza Corporation. You are probably familiar with them and possibly you've had a few of their pizzas. You see, I grew up in Ann Arbor, Michigan, which is the world headquarters of Domino's. Domino's was founded by Tom Monahan. He started the company as a young man when he walked into town with around $77 in his pocket and decided to open up a pizzeria. He opened it on the campus of a local University, where I went to school.

I don't know if there is anything that college students eat more of than pizza. There's no magic marketing strategy or research needed to indicate that there was a ready and hungry market, so naturally, there was a lot of competition. In doing his research, he asked himself "What problem could I solve to beat the competition?" He answered by saying, "If I deliver a hot, fresh pizza in 30 minutes or less, chances are they'll come back to me for another pizza. So, I'll make a guarantee that if it's not there in 30 minutes, the customer gets it free." Guess what? Instant UVP, with a seven second statement that became a mainstay in American households for years — "30 minutes or its free!" People took the challenge and tried to beat the system. If that pizza got there within 30 minutes, or even a little longer, and it was hot and fresh, they did come back for more. Although they gave away a free pizza once in awhile, it worked like magic, even in a highly competitive industry.

But it was more than that. Once they were hooked, people would come back out of a desire for comfort. In other words, the

For a FREE 7-day course on "7 Steps To Building A Successful Marketing Plan," send an e-mail to ChipTips@ChipCummings.com

77

competition couldn't just be *better*, they had to work twice as hard to overcome the "first-in wins" factor! Think about the first time that you moved into your neighborhood and ordered a pizza. If it was good, who did you call the next time, and the next, and the next? It doesn't matter what coupons came in the mail, if you liked that pizza, you were sold.

Tom Monahan knew that if he refined the experience so the customer enjoyed it, they would not only come back, but also tell their friends, frat buddies, and many other people on campus. As a result, he built that one location into thousands and thousands of stores around the world. His satisfied customers built his train into a mega-billion dollar business.

Recruit testimonials

In addition to personal, one-on-one referrals between the satisfied customers on your train and people they come in contact with, you should also recruit testimonials from your customers. A testimonial provides a powerful way for a customer to sing your praises, even when they aren't personally present. After you provide a great service to your client and build that relationship with trust, ask them to express in their own words what that experience has meant to them.

To recruit testimonials, develop a systematized approach. In my experience, I prep them for it way ahead of time, early in our relationship, and work my referral system in with the testimonial request. When I meet with a client the first time, I'll say, "I really appreciate that you stopped by today. I understand that Sue and John, your neighbors are the ones that suggested me. It's important to me, because the vast majority of my business comes from referrals. I look forward to helping not only you, but your family and friends. As you go through this transaction, if there's anything that's uncomfortable, I want you to tell me

For a FREE 7-day course on "7 Steps To Building A Successful Marketing Plan," send an e-mail to ChipTips@ChipCummings.com

78

immediately. It's important to me that you enjoy the same great experience Sue and John did. In the end, I'll ask you to honestly suggest ways I can improve. I'll ask you for some referrals when we're done, and also to provide a testimonial. I will share your testimonials with prospects so they can honestly judge the job I've done for others. Is that fair enough?"

This way, when we finish our dealings, there is no surprise. I make notes of what they tell me as we go through the transaction. At some point, I will say, "Did you enjoy everything? Do you have thoughts on ways I can improve? Fantastic! Over the next week, would you write down a few remarks about your experience? Before I stop by to pick up those comments, would you please look through your phone or contact list and give me three or four names of people that you feel would benefit from my service."

What are they doing for the next three or four days? Subconsciously they are thinking of names of friends, co-workers and family. They may talk to Pat at work or Chris at the grocery store. When they hear somebody says, "I was thinking of…" They will respond, "Oh, wow; I've got somebody; they are going to call me in a couple days and I'll ask them to contact you." They will come up with names and contacts out of the blue. This effect is similar to when you get a new car. Did you ever notice that there never seems to be very many of your type of car on the road — until you're driving one? Then they seem to be around every corner! Your subconscious level of awareness has been elevated.

When you call back to collect your testimonial, you are going to hear one of two responses. The first possible response will be something like, "Yeah, I talked to Chris down at the grocery store. Here's her name and number. She's expecting your call." Now, what have you just done? You've turned a cold call into a warm call. When I call Chris from the grocery store, my call is expected because a friend said I'd be calling. The second possible

For a FREE 7-day course on "7 Steps To Building A Successful Marketing Plan," send an e-mail to ChipTips@ChipCummings.com

79

response is "I haven't had time to write down the testimonial." When this happens, I offer a solution. I refer to those notes I took and suggest, "Since you are so busy, why don't I transcribe a few of your comments from the other day, and you simply sign it." Often people are delighted when I suggest this because it takes them off the spot. I've even developed a simpler solution using audio testimonials, which I will reveal to you in Chapter 10.

At the end of this book, I'll ask you for your testimonial! This will give me a chance to let other companies and customers read about the impact my key points made in improving your results, and I will offer you a valuable gift in return!

Follow-up with "personal touches"

Another component in the Rule of Reach is the necessity to stay in contact. People will not stay attached to your "train" (i.e. give you referrals), unless you stay in touch and allow them to still feel connected to you. You must provide four to six personal "touches" with a customer per year. Four is the absolute minimum.

What is the penalty if you ignore those four personal touches per year? The customer is not yours. They may go elsewhere. They will probably not even remember your name. Remember the study that indicated that less than 10 percent of respondents could remember the name of their loan officer after one year. The result stunned most people in my industry and it should scare the devil out of you. Stay in touch.

Work to ensure you're in the 10 percent that are remembered by their customers. Contact clients four to six times each year through automation and technology. I'm not talking about just personal phone calls. That's one possibility, but you can use e-mails, faxes, letters, conference calls, newsletters, e-zines, or sponsored events. Contact them so your name remains in front of them. These personal touches are not intended as a request for

For a FREE 7-day course on "7 Steps To Building A Successful Marketing Plan," send an e-mail to ChipTips@ChipCummings.com

80

repeat business. Instead, they should demonstrate that you remember them and you continue to care.

There are many creative ways you can contact customers and the contact doesn't have to take place "one at a time." As an example, when my client base grew to over 8,000 customers, I knew it would be difficult to maintain contact unless we took a different approach. My staff came up with an ingenious idea. We figured out a way to get most of our previous clients together at one time. We rented out the entire bleacher section at the baseball park of a Triple-A ball club, the West Michigan Whitecaps, and handed out 5,000 tickets to our customers. Our past clients and their families came out on a Sunday afternoon and enjoyed a day at the ballpark. Did they see it as a sales call? No! But, I created thousands of personal touches with just one event, and energized my Evangelists!

Leverage your time

If you're building your train based on providing only your own time, you inevitably limit how long your train can become. You can still engage the customer in a great experience even if you aren't there 100 percent of the time. The trick is to find other engineers, conductors, and stewards to help run your train in the same fashion as you have so carefully designed. These will be your trusted team members, and as I previously mentioned, it is in your best interest to make sure they know where the train is going!

To illustrate the dynamics of building a team, I was talking to a salon owner who told me, "There's a gentleman I know that's able to charge $250 for a haircut." I was shocked, "Two hundred and fifty bucks for a haircut? Where?"

The owner replied, "He happens to be in New York City,

For a FREE 7-day course on "7 Steps To Building A Successful Marketing Plan," send an e-mail to ChipTips@ChipCummings.com

81

but people come to him from all over for his name and because of his technique."

"How does he do it? Does he spend a lot of time with each customer?"

He replied, "No; he spends exactly 15 minutes with every customer."

I laugh, "A haircut takes longer than that especially if I'm paying $250."

The Salon owner smiled, "Yes; there is a separate specialist that comes in to shampoo, color the hair, give the head massage and other things. After they leave, there is someone else that dries it a little bit, puts some stuff in it; then in walks the specialist. He looks at it, does some clips, spends 15 minutes and says, 'Okay,' and then he's off to the next one. Then another associate blow dries the hair and does the final touches. It's a system."

The $250 hairdresser figured out that as long as the customer knows he is in control, fifteen minutes spent with his customers is enough. This is the same concept used for doctors, dentists, attorneys, CFP's, CPA's, and any provider of professional business services! You however, have to make sure you provide enough "face time" for your customers' expectations. This will vary depending on the service provided, and the nature of the transaction, but you get to set the standards! When it's not enough, your customer base will let you know.

As an example, one loan broker told me, "I do a lot of loans and I have an assistant, so I tried having the assistant do a lot more in the loan process. After I conducted client surveys, I found out that people were saying they didn't have enough contact with me. That really shook me because I realized that I can do a big volume of business if I have a support staff, but I have to use the time it frees up to concentrate on more client interaction. So now, I spend a few more minutes on the front end

For a FREE 7-day course on "7 Steps To Building A Successful Marketing Plan," send an e-mail to ChipTips@ChipCummings.com

82

setting the tone, and on a client's move-in date, I show up at their door with a welcome basket. Not only did it increase customer confidence in the transaction, but it has drastically increased the number of referrals as well!"

Her customers are now walking billboards, inviting family and friends to hitch a ride on her train. If she hadn't done that last bit of research, she never would have known how they felt about her, and they eventually would have stopped referring business to her.

Listen to what your customers are saying. If you're dealing with a first time customer, they may need more handholding than somebody who has been through this experience 16 times. First time customers are more likely to send in a survey that says, "I didn't see you enough. I didn't hear enough. I need to have that reassurance." When you get customers that have used your services several times, you don't have to spend as much face time with them. In effect, they say, "I know you're there to provide certain things and you're overseeing. I don't need to talk to you unless there's a problem."

Think about your niche and how you're going to allot that "face" time. Spend more time in the beginning of the process so the customer feels comfortable. Explain the fact that you are going to have an assistant speaking with them but you'll oversee the solution. You need to convey, "I'm in control of the transaction. I'll be watching everything my people do, and Mr. and Mrs. Customer, if you ever have any concern or question whatsoever, I want you to pick up the phone and call me personally; OK?"

Follow these guidelines, and you will have set up the foundation of the Rule of Reach — connecting with people in a relationship building, trustworthy atmosphere. One in which you will own the biggest, badest train anyone has every seen! Now let's put it into drive, and dig into some specific marketing strategies!

For a FREE 7-day course on "7 Steps To Building A Successful Marketing Plan," send an e-mail to ChipTips@ChipCummings.com

83

CHIP TIPS:

Here are your "personal road signs" from this Chapter:

1. Each business only has three types of customers: past, present and future. Depending on your target market niche and group, you will use different methods to reach each of these groups.

2. Always think in terms of relational marketing rather than transactional marketing.

3. Remember the Rule of the Four R's: Research, React, Respect and Referrals. These rules establish the basic system you'll use to determine your niche and reach past, present and future customers.

4. Ask questions, listen carefully, and figure out if you have a solution that is in the customers' best interest.

5. Expect to make six to seven customer contacts before someone will decide to buy from you.

6. Define the customer experience by mapping out the entire process from the customer's first impressions to referral machine (i.e. Evangelist).

7. Referrals are the key to your business. Ask for a testimonial early in the relationship with your customers.

8. Make at least four "personal touches" with your customers each year.

For a FREE 7-day course on "7 Steps To Building A Successful Marketing Plan," send an e-mail to ChipTips@ChipCummings.com

84

Chapter 6

The Secrets of Profitable Websites

"Creative thinking may mean simply the realization that there's no particular virtue in doing things the way they've always been done."

Rudolf Flesch

One of the cornerstones of your business is your website. A website is your second most important marketing tool, eclipsed by only you personally. Nothing will ever replace the power of one-on-one personal "face time" with a customer or prospect in building a relationship, but a website is a close second. If you do not have a website, you must get one. It is a personal extension of you and your business, and you cannot operate a business today without one. Unfortunately, most people use them in the wrong way.

Your website acts as an interactive brochure, publishing platform, and invitation for permission marketing, all available 24 hours a day, seven days a week, 365 days a year. It is the best sales employee you will ever have, as it doesn't ask for raises, vacation pay or time off. It allows customers and prospects to reach your business instantly from anywhere in the world, and if you have a customer who does their business at 2 A.M. and they want to learn about your product, your website provides a way to answer their questions while you sleep.

For a FREE 7-day course on "7 Steps To Building A Successful Marketing Plan," send an e-mail to ChipTips@ChipCummings.com

85

It doesn't matter if you work for a large company, a small firm, or are a one-person operation — everyone can compete on a level playing field, the field that comprises about 15" of monitor space on a prospect's desktop. This is an extension of you and your product/service, so don't take this task lightly. According to Forrester Research, 40% of website visitors do not return to a site if their first visit results in a negative experience! Make it count. There is a right way and a wrong way to implement a website, but the only thing better than a badly designed website is no website at all.

If you plan to develop a website yourself, it's best if you have some design experience. However, since that is not the best use of your time and energy however, you should consider hiring a professional website designer, preferably one that has some marketing experience. As you would do in selecting a new vehicle, you don't need to know exactly how every part under the hood works, but you do need to know the basics of the engine, what makes it run, and select the color and options you want to reflect your personality.

In planning out your website (which could be one single page or hundreds), it is important to map it out, and map out the strategies you will use to attract, capture and convert visitors — BEFORE you hire or consult a web designer. Let's take a look at the basics of building your marketing engine.

Planning your site

I own, manage and control over 150 different websites and domains. They exist for a wide variety of purposes, but most run on "autopilot" which means they don't require any effort or upkeep. The idea is to set it up and let it run. While I have learned a great deal, and do know the basics of design and implementation, I am a marketing specialist by nature and

For a FREE 7-day course on "7 Steps To Building A Successful Marketing Plan," send an e-mail to ChipTips@ChipCummings.com

86

concentrate on the strategies themselves. I have found that ANYTHING you can imagine can be created and done with a website. But, I always start each project the same way — by mapping it out. By doing a good thorough job in the beginning, it will mean a lot less time, expense and frustration later on.

As simple and basic as it seems, you need to start by thoroughly planning out the website. For many professions and industries, there are loads of "pre-fab" template website construction models available, so I use these models as a foundation from which to start. Think of these templates as the "back room" or operational component of your on-line store.

Several years back, I looked at developing an entire site for my mortgage operation from scratch, but even with basic features and calculators, the estimate came to a whopping $70,000! Now of course, you can get the same features for less than $2000. It doesn't matter what business you are in — don't try to re-invent the wheel. To develop a good basic website should not cost you more than that, but the more time you put into planning, the more money you will save. There are others in your industry that have spent the money and developed the ideas and concepts. Being unique will only lead to greater expense, and problems with implementation and future upgrades.

Start by "surfing" the Internet, and looking at competitor's sites and other related industries. Test them out and make a list of the sites and features that you like. Think carefully about how your customers will use the site as well! Remember that this is a marketing tool first, operational tool second.

As you start to construct your "wish list" of design features, just concentrate on the main website page. For most smaller companies and individual salespeople, the web templates are a great way to go to save time and money. But that is the operational side — you want to control the front door. For example, I can purchase and use a pre-designed template for taking mortgage loan applications,

For a FREE 7-day course on "7 Steps To Building A Successful Marketing Plan," send an e-mail to ChipTips@ChipCummings.com

87

posting interest rates, payment calculators, rent-to-own investment analysis features, etc. and still have a "web shell" or front page of which I control the look and feel. This allows me to implement the marketing strategies I desire, and I can construct various web-links to pages or parts of the operational template in the back of the store!

As I develop and "map out" a website, here is the list of initial mandatory items:

1. **It must be easy to find.** I know that I need to develop a naming strategy that includes an easy-to-remember domain name and any obvious misspellings.

2. **It must be "clean."** The site must be easy to read and use. If they want to apply for a loan, I don't want them hunting to find the right place to click, or have to click several times to reach what they need.

3. **It must work with current applications.** If I am capturing data in any pages or fields, I need to make sure that information and the applications work seamlessly with any of my internal operational systems and my business software. My on-line applications must be able to import directly into my origination program with one click. Inquiries for real estate agents, insurance professionals, architects, attorneys or other businesses must be able to directly import data into their database systems.

4. **It must satisfy the 7-second rule.** I assume that I only have 7 seconds to capture the customers' interest when they visit my site, so I design the site accordingly. I'll cover this rule in more depth later in this chapter.

5. **It must be easy to navigate.** Is it attractive, understandable and easy to use? Don't "buck the trend" — keep the navigation bars on the left and/or top, and use blue web-links. Can an 8-yr.old navigate it? According to a study done by NetSmart Research, 83% of web users have left sites in

For a FREE 7-day course on "7 Steps To Building A Successful Marketing Plan," send an e-mail to ChipTips@ChipCummings.com

88

frustration due to poor usability. Unintuitive navigation and sluggish performance were mentioned as the main culprits!

6. **It must be easy for them to contact me.** I include e-mail links, company address, and phone numbers on every page, and in several places on the site.

Six rules for creating effective websites

After working with thousands of companies and sales professionals over the years, and personally creating and testing hundreds of web page strategies, I found there are six basic rules for creating an effective website. Follow this formula, and you will generate great success with your customers. Break the rules, and it could be a very expensive lesson!

1. Playing the Name Game

If you needed to locate a complete stranger by tomorrow, could you do it? Suppose they had some specialized product or service that you had to have, but you had nothing more than simply a name. What would you do first? Call information? Check the newspaper or Yellow Pages? How about the Internet?

It's no secret that more and more people are turning to the Internet for fast, easy access to information. But if your customers need to find you, have you ever stopped to wonder how easy (or difficult) that might be? As businesspeople, we spend thousands of dollars making sure that customers and potential clients know our names. We advertise in newspapers, phone books, local radio, TV, and use all sorts of other gimmicks to create an identity in the marketplace so people will call us first. But what have we missed?

If someone hears the name "Chip Cummings" in the marketplace, can they find me right away? Where might they

For a FREE 7-day course on "7 Steps To Building A Successful Marketing Plan," send an e-mail to ChipTips@ChipCummings.com

89

start? If they use an Internet search engine like Google, MSN or Yahoo, they are going to type in "Chip Cummings." Guess what? If a "Cummings" pops up who is my competitor, I possibly lost business, didn't I?

If someone happened to hear at a party, "Chip Cummings is a great lender. Chip solved my problem and got us into our new house." The listener thinks, "I've got to remember that name." Hopefully they write it down, but what if they spelled it "Skip Cummings?" Well, if they type "Skip Cummings" into a search engine, guess what? They still find my website because I learned how to play the Name Game.

The Name Game is about making sure that you are found on the Internet even if someone misspells your name or knows very little about you. How do you do that? Plan to search for yourself on the Internet. Take this simple test. Go to www.Google.com and type your name into the "Search" box. What results will the search engine show? Now type your company name in, or better yet, enter your city + {your business}. For example, if you are a mortgage broker you might type in "Cleveland+Mortgages". Now try the same thing at www.MSN.com, www.Ask.com and www.Yahoo.com (these are a few of the most popular search sites). Is your name or website even listed?

In Chapter 7, we'll look at strategies in more detail about how you can build name variations into your website, but right now start by making a note of every way your target audience might spell your name and the name of your business.

Master your domain

As you strategize about your customer's experience, start off with the domain name. Search engines will first look for actual website addresses that match the search request input by a customer, so that's where you need to start. The Internet *domain*

For a FREE 7-day course on "7 Steps To Building A Successful Marketing Plan," send an e-mail to ChipTips@ChipCummings.com

90

name is your address on the Internet. Similar to a physical postal address, no two entities can own the same exact domain name. The part of the domain name after the period (i.e. .com, .net, .org, etc.) is called the *top-level domain name*. It was designed to help organize websites into categories such as those for commerce (.com), schools (.edu), organizations (.org), etc.

When setting up your domain name, make it simple and memorable. While there are many other top-level domain names to choose from, start with a dot-com extension with the simple spelling of your company name whenever possible. Customers will not check other extensions such as .biz, .net, .org, etc. Think about it, if you wanted to find information about a BMW automobile, where is the first place you would look? BMW.com, right?

You should immediately reserve your personal name as a domain name, such as JohnThompson.com. When someone is looking for me, they will naturally find me at www.ChipCummings.com. If your own name is already taken, then go for a variation such as TheJohnThompson.com, or DrJohnT.com. A great resource for searching and reserving domain names at very low cost is www.InstantCheapDomains.com. If I am an individual salesperson, I can then FORWARD this URL address into the main company website page, or any other location — similar to call-forwarding for a telephone.

To check and see if any name is available, go to InstantCheapDomains.com and just type in the name. You can also check out a comprehensive list of recently expired domain names at www.whois.net or www.pool.com. It is quite inexpensive (about $8 per year) to register a name, so register your own personal name for a 10 year period, and your company name for at least 5 years. When your registration period expires, the registrar will automatically notify you to renew your domain

For a FREE 7-day course on "7 Steps To Building A Successful Marketing Plan," send an e-mail to ChipTips@ChipCummings.com

91

registration. If you fail to re-register, then your domain name becomes "public property" again at which time someone else can snatch it up, so make sure you keep on top of your registrations.

Anticipate misspellings

Many people don't know how to spell, or can make simple typing errors. Play the game. Not only did I reserve the correct spelling of my own name, I also own several other domain names that anticipate someone misspelling my name or the name of my company. Perhaps they only spell my last name with one "M," or they forget a "G." In all those cases, with web forwarding, they are still being redirected to my website.

There are a lot of companies that have names that are difficult to spell. I attended a seminar once in which the presenter, Mr. Zimanabek, asked the attendees to attempt to spell his name. Participants couldn't spell it correctly, and hacked it up pretty good. Make sure that if your target audience misspells your name, they are still going to find you.

This applies to your company name also. This is particularly important if your company name is difficult to spell like "Pierson Mortgage." Is that "Peer?" Is that "Pear?" How many different ways are people going to spell it? Own as many spelling combinations as you can and then forward them directly to your main site. Reserve the misspellings for a 1 year period, and track the click-throughs to determine exactly how many people are typing it incorrectly. If you get a significant number of re-directs from that misspelling, then keep it and renew that domain name.

Because I "listen" to the ways my customers might attempt to reach me, I control around 90 different website names just for tracking misspellings. For example, in my industry, I can't afford to assume people know how to spell "mortgage." It's written as "morgage," "morgag," "mortgige," "mortage," and other ways.

For a FREE 7-day course on "7 Steps To Building A Successful Marketing Plan," send an e-mail to ChipTips@ChipCummings.com

92

So "Pierson Mortgage," for example, might also own "Peerson Mortgage", "Pearson Mortgage" and several other combinations of those misspellings.

One other strategy to let you in on in playing the name game. If you are a high-profile individual, celebrity-type, or larger more visible company, then also reserve names that are on the "dark side." Actual websites are created to annoy and divert attention, and can be counter-productive to you and your company. There are actual sites for www.(name)sucks.com and other variations. When necessary, it's better that you control those variations rather than your competition or unruly customers. You don't need to forward them anywhere, just own them.

Use web forwarding

So you now have one website, but multiple registered domain names. What do you do to make sure people get to your website regardless of which domain name they type? The answer is web forwarding. When you register with most domain registrars, they typically also offer a service that allows you to forward from your domain name to another domain or any Uniform Resource Locator (URL). This service is free at www.InstantCheapDomains.com. The URL describes the exact location on the Internet where your website can be found, similar to a file path on a PC. For example, your domain name may be JoeSmith.com, but you may forward people to http://www.comcast.net~JoeSmith/.

This is particularly useful if you are associated with the website of a larger organization. For example, if I was working with another mortgage company, my web host could point my ChipCummings.com to the company website or a particular page within that site. Later, if I switch companies, I can simply reroute my domain name to another URL. It will automatically send my clients where I want them to go, without having to change my domain name.

For a FREE 7-day course on "7 Steps To Building A Successful Marketing Plan," send an e-mail to ChipTips@ChipCummings.com

93

2. Designing the experience

In Chapter 5, we discussed designing and creating the perfect customer experience. You have to extend that same theory to your website. Look at your website objectively. Pretend you are your own customer and imagine what you would want to find the first time you visited your site. What is the first thing that your website is asking you to do? Where is your attention drawn to? Have a friend from outside your industry tell you what they notice and what they are first inclined to do once they are at your site.

If you need inspiration, visit one of your competitor's websites. You can learn much from what they do right and wrong. For example, I once visited a competitor's website to see how easy it was to apply for a loan. The site was so overloaded with poorly organized content that I get lost in all the verbiage. I had to click through four or five screens just to get to the correct form to fill out. If I'm one of their potential customers I'm now wondering if the rest of the process is as confusing, or complicated as finding that form. As a result, and fortunately for me, that company probably misses a lot of potential customers.

The lesson I learned from this exercise is that if I'm a customer and I go to apply for a mortgage on a website, I expect to see a button on the first page that displays, "Apply for a loan here." I'm confident that if I click there, I am applying for a loan. It's easy and reassuring. If a client visits my website, they don't care about me. They want to know what I can do for them. They are interested in my loan programs and rates, plus how to apply for money. Don't make it about you; make your site about how your customer can solve their problem with your assistance.

Why are your customers seeking you out? I hate websites where you see a picture of someone's building. Who cares what their building looks like? Would you buy from someone based on the building they work in? This is where listening to your

For a FREE 7-day course on "7 Steps To Building A Successful Marketing Plan," send an e-mail to ChipTips@ChipCummings.com

94

customer during your research is going to pay off. What do they want to learn once they get to your website, and what possible courses of action could they take once they get that information?

3. Seven second rule

Remember earlier when we developed our seven second statement? Well this is why I told you to spend some time working on that! Similarly, on the Internet, you don't have a lot of time to capture the customer's attention. Once a potential client finds your home page, you have only a few seconds to do two things: convince them they found the right place and give them what they came to find. If the visitor is overwhelmed or uncertain, they may click off your website and look for another site which is easier to use.

Make sure customers know they have found the correct website. Whether they identify it by your name, your business, or an instantly recognizable logo, your client must be able to recognize they've come to the right place. You must also quickly convince them they can actually do what they came there to do.

For example, in my case, a client should be able to tell a friend, "I went to ChipCummings.com to apply for a loan. As soon as I opened the site, I clicked on the application." They knew immediately it was my site and quickly spotted what they wanted. Will a visitor to your site find it identifiable and easy to use?

Visit your competitors' websites. You will find some really bad examples out there. Others are clean, concise, and easy-to-read. Those sites capture customers. Learn from the bad material and steal good ideas from the best.

Make sure the "download time" of the site, the time it takes to appear in the window is relatively fast. Test it on a slow dial-up modem speed to be sure! According to a study performed by the

For a FREE 7-day course on "7 Steps To Building A Successful Marketing Plan," send an e-mail to ChipTips@ChipCummings.com

95

Boston Consulting Group, almost 70% of online consumers reported that some websites take too long to download. Don't make your Prospects wait!

4. Eight-year-old rule

Make sure your website is simple to read and easy to navigate. You can test this by applying what I call the Eight-Year-Old Rule. This one actually comes from my daughter, Katelyn.

When she was young, I noticed the websites Katelyn visited were more interesting than many regular business sites. Knowing that they targeted children, the designers applied simple language and style. You can learn from these examples. Adults want to read and understand your website just as easily. Test your website with a child. Find out what their attention is drawn to, and ask them what they are first inclined to do once they get there. Ask them to do a specific task, like "what would you do if you wanted to apply for a loan?" If an eight-year-old can navigate your site, you're all right. If you need a Ph.D. to navigate your website, you've got a problem.

Want some ideas of how to create simple websites? Go to the sites that kids visit. Study the concepts. They are often not glitzy, or flashy. Look at Disney, Nickelodeon, or Nick at Nite. They use simple pictures, and are easy to navigate for somebody with basic skills.

Avoid using jargon or acronyms. In my industry, I'd never put, "Click here for a 1003" (a frequently used form). People in my industry don't always know what that means so you should not assume your customer will. Put your message in plain English so even a child can read it. If you think I'm over simplifying, remember, virtually all TV newscasts are written to the level of an eighth grade audience.

For a FREE 7-day course on "7 Steps To Building A Successful Marketing Plan," send an e-mail to ChipTips@ChipCummings.com

96

5. Capture rule

Despite what you may think or what you've been told, your website really exists for one primary purpose: to capture a name and e-mail address. That is the most important result your website can produce. Yes, you're going to provide some information there, offer products, have calculators or other operational features, but unless they have been driven there to place an order (through some other type of response trigger), that is not your main purpose.

I recently had a potential client proudly inform me that they had over 1,000,000 visitors to their website last month. I politely asked how many sales he made, how many people were added to his mailing list or customer database, and how he was following up on those one million visitors. He got real quiet.

Through effective listening, you'll learn the information that attracts customers to your website. When you provide what they want and they visit, you'll know they fit your target market. They are probably a well-qualified suspect, and your purpose is to convert them into a prospect. The only way you can do that is if you have a way to get back in touch with them.

You can't contact them if you don't have at least their name and e-mail address or phone number. Design your website to capture their contact information. In chapter 7, I will give you some specific ways to create Personal Value, as well as how to create the "Ethical Bribe" — trading value for their name and e-mail address!

Using pop-ups

One basic strategy you can use to capture website visitor contact information is with pop-ups. Yes, I know they're intrusive, they're annoying, and they bug everyone-but they work!

Anyone who's spent more than 2 minutes on the Internet has probably seen a "pop-up." You know, those often annoying little

For a FREE 7-day course on "7 Steps To Building A Successful Marketing Plan," send an e-mail to ChipTips@ChipCummings.com

97

ads that seem to pop-up right in the middle of your screen pitching everything from new cars to the latest medical breakthroughs. But if there are a lot of companies using the technique, then that tells you something-it must be working. The trick is *how* you use them!

First, understand that a "pop-up" is nothing more than a mini website page that appears over (or under) the page you are viewing. The mini-web page is triggered to open automatically when you visit a certain website or web page. The concept is widely used (and misused) for advertising purposes.

A recent survey conducted by AOL indicates that 86% of all Internet users found pop-ups either "somewhat or very annoying." I have to admit I'm also in that group. But a closer look at the statistics reveals that the main reasons that people find them so intrusive is due to the timing and/or content of the pop-up (92%). People don't like to be inundated with *multiple* pop-ups, and the content must be relevant to what they are searching for!

With all the pop-up blockers available now, you might assume everyone would use this software to suppress pop-ups. However, studies show that, even though they are heavily promoted, pop-up blocker software is used by only 14 percent of people using the Internet. So, why doesn't everyone use pop-up blocker software? Because that software can't distinguish between an advertisement and useful information. Since a pop-up is nothing more than another web page, a person may disable or avoid using a pop-up blocker so they don't miss important information that may appear in a pop-up, such as an application form. You can also use other web page "call" techniques that bring up a related web page, but are not recognized by pop-up blockers. So knowing what the consumer does and doesn't want, let's take a look at how we can use this technique to increase the capture rate and conversion of our potential customers.

For a FREE 7-day course on "7 Steps To Building A Successful Marketing Plan," send an e-mail to ChipTips@ChipCummings.com

98

Pop-up strategies

Remember that the main purpose of your website is to capture and convert the visitor into a prospect. So, you want to provide a forum to get their name and e-mail address and drive them into your system or to your sales team for future follow-up. Pop-ups allow you to focus their attention in a specific area, and react in a logical way (such as clicking for more information) when it's relevant to their interest.

As an example, in my industry, if a customer is searching for information about 100% financing or first-time home buyer programs, a pop-up could offer a free special report (see example below) that matches their interest and is delivered immediately. If they are looking at a builder's website, maybe a pop-up could offer a free pre-construction consultation, or a report on "How to Avoid the 4 Biggest Mistakes Most People Make When Constructing A New Home."

For First-Time Homebuyers!

Find out the *7 things* you need to know BEFORE buying your First Home! Click Here For Your Free Report

No Obligation!

You can also use pop-ups as a tie-in with specific affiliates that you work with. For example, a strategic link within a real estate website could display financing information without having to leave the real estate agent's main web page. This strategy also works well with CPA's, financial planners, attorneys, insurance agents, architects and builders.

The key is that the pop-up itself has to be *information* based. It must be directly related to the purpose of their visit. In other words, don't use a pop-up for interest rates on a website advertising women's clothing!

The pop-up must also be well-timed for a positive reaction. It's probably best not to hit them with a pop-up the second they

For a FREE 7-day course on "7 Steps To Building A Successful Marketing Plan," send an e-mail to ChipTips@ChipCummings.com

99

pull up your home page! As long as you have good content, a method to capture their contact information, and the proper timing and placement of the pop-up itself, your customer will respond positively most of the time. As a general rule, DO NOT put a pop-up on the main page of your website. Not only will this be viewed as annoying, it will most likely get you banned from the search engines.

Types of pop-ups

You can trigger pop-ups to appear *over* the page that they are currently viewing (pop-over), or *under* the page (known as a pop-under). Over the page pop-ups are the traditional kind we're all used to seeing. Under the page pop-ups (also known as "pop-unders"), actually display underneath the currently viewed web browser window. You won't see the pop-up until you close out of the browser. This way, the pop-up doesn't intrude on the customer's experience, but appears as they leave so we get our point across one last time.

If your pop-up has to do with newsletter sign-ups or exit surveys from an affiliate site, the pop-under works better. If the pop-up contains relevant information website visitors are asking for or related to their web page request (applications, programs, forms, etc.), then the pop-over would be your best choice.

Using delayed pop-ups, you can also employ a timing strategy which delays the pop-up from appearing for 5, 10, or 30 seconds, or even for hours! Delayed pop-ups are best suited for reminders, second chances, or affiliated strategic partner reports such as "The 8 Biggest Tax-saving Strategies That Most Homeowners Miss," provided by your CPA.

Smart pop-ups remember if the customer requested that information before. This way you don't display the same pop-up for information that the customer has already requested. You can

For a FREE 7-day course on "7 Steps To Building A Successful Marketing Plan," send an e-mail to ChipTips@ChipCummings.com

100

also use a "pop-up rotator" which switches between different offers each time your web page comes up. This allows you to test how well each pop-up is working relative to other pop-ups.

Yet another variation is called an "exit pop-up." The difference between this type and the pop-under is that this pop-up moves immediately to the front as soon as the customer leaves the site to visit another website. Whereas, you can't see a pop-under until you close the browser. This is useful for a last shot at trying to capture the customer before they leave. For example, if a customer visits my page on construction loans, when they leave my site a pop-up emerges saying, "FREE — Three Tips to Selecting the Best Builder." That alternative may grab them. If I didn't get them once, it gives me a chance to take one more shot before they leave.

Whichever strategies you use, remember to test your pop-ups for customer reaction, using different timing, content, colors, positioning and response triggers.

Implementing pop-ups

Since I am not exactly a techno-wizard, I have always strived to keep these strategies simple. Start with just one simple pop-up for a free report or e-newsletter to capture a name and e-mail address from visitors on your main web page.

Although I have created hundreds of pop-ups and coached many others on these techniques, I realize that the first one is the hardest to create. I've never tried to create one totally from scratch-I use simple software programs for that! The two best programs I have used are from Instant Attention (www.InstantStickyNotes.com) and Pop-Up Generator (www.PopoverGenerator.com). Programs like these cost anywhere from $29 to $79. They include hundreds of pre-made templates and instructional videos. Typically, you can

For a FREE 7-day course on "7 Steps To Building A Successful Marketing Plan," send an e-mail to ChipTips@ChipCummings.com

101

create a pop-up with these software products in about 10 minutes. These programs also allow you to create pop-ups which are "smarter" and configured for maximum viewing exposure even for Internet users who use pop-up blockers. Another cleaver program I have used which defies pop-up blockers is the Opt-in Automator (www.OptinAutomator.com/x.cgi?id=72186) Once you create the pop-up, then just forward it to your website designer, or slip it into the site yourself! These types of pop-ups have been designed to get past any pop-up blocker in the world!

Pop-ups when properly and respectfully used can enhance the customer's web visit experience, and increase the capture and conversion rate of your visitors. And without a happy visitor, you'll never get to convert them to a happy client!

For a FREE 7-day course on "7 Steps To Building A Successful Marketing Plan," send an e-mail to ChipTips@ChipCummings.com

102

CHIP TIPS:

Here are your "personal road signs" from this Chapter:

1. "Map out" your website so that it is easy to find, cleanly designed, works with current applications, satisfies the 7-second rule, easy to navigate, and provides easy contact information.

2. Register a domain name for your personal name and your company name, as well as any misspellings.

3. Design your website to capture the visitors' attention within seven seconds, and make it simple enough that an eight-year-old can navigate the site without a problem.

4. The most important function of your website is to capture a name and e-mail address, so be sure to make it comfortable for visitors to give you their contact information.

5. Use pop-ups. As long as you have good content, a method to capture their contact information, and the proper timing and placement of the pop-up itself, your customer will respond positively most of the time.

For a FREE 7-day course on "7 Steps To Building A Successful Marketing Plan," send an e-mail to ChipTips@ChipCummings.com

103

For a FREE 7-day course on "7 Steps To Building A Successful Marketing Plan," send an e-mail to ChipTips@ChipCummings.com

104

Chapter 7

Traffic Generation and Conversion

"Action may not always bring happiness, but there is no happiness without action."

Benjamin Disraeli

I t's time to hit the road at full speed. As an extension of the "Rule of Reach", we now take a look at key strategies for driving traffic to your website and then converting them from Suspects to Prospects.

From Suspects to Evangelists

Before we discuss how you use your website to capture Prospects, let's review the evolution customers go through as they engage your business. As I discussed in the Anatomy of A Customer, if you do things right, customers will evolve from Suspects to Evangelists.

Suspects. This is your target audience. If you've done the research we talked about in Chapter 5, you should know this audience well. This will become important as we research the search patterns of your target audience on the Internet.

For a FREE 7-day course on "7 Steps To Building A Successful Marketing Plan," send an e-mail to ChipTips@ChipCummings.com

105

Prospects. These are people who you believe are good candidates to become clients. You have caught their attention, and have some amount of personal contact information, so you can engage in a direct conversation with them. You might get their contact information through a lead or because they provided their e-mail address on your website to get a free report. As we'll discuss later in this chapter, moving customers from suspects to prospect is the main goal of your website.

Clients. These are people who trust you enough to actually buy something from you. You may think you are done when people reach this point, but, as we discussed in previous chapters, this is just the beginning. By providing outstanding service, you can move clients to the next evolutionary stage.

Evangelists. Due to the exceptional attention you've paid to them, these clients are such fans of your business that they go out of their way to tell their friends, family, and colleagues. They will provide a renewable source of leads, building long-term success.

Again, as you'll see in the rest of this chapter, since your energy should be focused on the Customer/Evangelist side of the equation, we will use technology and your website as your main tool for moving suspects to prospects and even further up the evolutionary chain.

Your Central Marketing Tool

In Chapter 6, we covered much about planning and building your website. Here we reinforce the fact that your website really exists for one purpose and one purpose only: to capture a name and e-mail address.

To do that, you have to accomplish two things. First, you have to make it easy for your suspects to find you. Second, you have

For a FREE 7-day course on "7 Steps To Building A Successful Marketing Plan," send an e-mail to ChipTips@ChipCummings.com

106

For a FREE 7-day course on "7 Steps To Building A Successful Marketing Plan," send an e-mail to ChipTips@ChipCummings.com

107

to convince them to give you their e-mail address (i.e. convert them into prospects).

Technically, your website is your #2 marketing tool because YOU are the #1 marketing tool. Nothing will ever replace the personal touch, style or comfort you are able to deliver through "face time" with a client. But, reality is, you can't personally meet with or qualify 1000 potential or current clients in a day. However, technology can. Positioned correctly, your website can provide a steady stream of warm prospects and happy clients.

You must realize that your website is a marketing tool, not just an online brochure. As I meet and speak to thousands of people across the country, I am constantly amazed to find that many use their site as a *business tool*, but not as a *marketing tool*! Just like any other marketing tool, your website needs to be tested and adjusted based on the *client's* expectations (not yours).

To turn it into an effective *marketing* tool, you need to master two concepts: targeting traffic and traffic conversion.

Targeting traffic

I always get a kick out of people that tell me they had "1 million hits last month on my website" or "7,000 unique visitors." They have a different answer when I ask them how many became direct customers. Frankly, the "visitor" numbers don't mean a thing. I could place an expensive billboard along the freeway in Los Angeles, have 200,000 people see it, and it wouldn't mean a thing if I were advertising mortgages in Michigan. It just doesn't make any marketing sense. So why should your website be any different?

I would gladly give up 1,000,000 website visitors who have little to no interest in my services for 1,000 highly targeted qualified visits. It's the same concept as placing an ad in a section of your local paper vs. The Wall Street Journal!

For a FREE 7-day course on "7 Steps To Building A Successful Marketing Plan," send an e-mail to ChipTips@ChipCummings.com

108

For customers, the whole driving concept behind the Internet is instant gratification of information on their terms (i.e. convenience). So the question is, how do you drive *targeted* traffic to your site? The answer: appeal to their desire for information in the most likely place to find your target suspects.

As an example, if I were marketing my services to first-time homebuyers, I would create a series of special reports that explain important topics specifically directed to that target market. These might include:

+ How you can get into a home with no money and no credit

+ Understanding your credit report and the credit scoring process

+ Understanding the home-buying process

+ How to select interest rates and loan programs

In any professional services industry, or with products that are unique or have a higher market value, the only differentiating factor you can bring to the table is your professional experience and expertise. Smaller products and lower ticket items are usually bought by consumers based on convenience, not price or service. There are competitors that can offer the exact same item or service, at the same price or lower, so you have to create a different kind of value — Personal Value.

Creating Personal Value

Personal Value, or "Chip Value" as I call it, is the single greatest marketing weapon you possess. People want information, and they want it in an organized, easy-to-understand and instantly accessible format from an experienced professional. After all, that's what drives the entire Internet. The

For a FREE 7-day course on "7 Steps To Building A Successful Marketing Plan," send an e-mail to ChipTips@ChipCummings.com

109

size of your client database (and your profits) are directly related to how well you are able to communicate this information as it relates to their personal needs.

As an experienced professional in your industry, you have a world of information to share — from the financial sector, it might be how to understand credit reports, or explaining the different costs associated in a loan transaction. For builders or construction specialists it might be how to save money by using different types of building materials or the pitfalls of cost overruns.

But your "value" doesn't stop there! You also have contact with a host of other affiliated professionals that most people don't get easy access to — different suppliers and vendors such as appraisers, surveyors, underwriters, title insurers, and others for the real estate world just as an example. The secret is to convert your information resources to a deliverable format for potential or existing clients. The answer is in creating free reports.

Free reports (sometimes known as "White Papers"), come from one of two perspectives — direct personal experience, or the knowledge of affiliate partner experts. Start by making a list of the top 5 things (questions, issues, problems, etc.) that your customers ask you about on a regular basis. In my industry these probably include topics such as interest rates, closing costs, credit, income or employment, various loan programs, and many others. Next, make a list of the top 5 most important things that your target market wants to know about that is *related* to your industry. Again, using real estate finance as an example, this may include subjects such as understanding the home construction process, home maintenance and safety, tax planning strategies, moving tips, shopping for a real estate agent, or how to protect yourself from identity theft. Once you have the topics in place, it's time to create some simple reports.

For a FREE 7-day course on "7 Steps To Building A Successful Marketing Plan," send an e-mail to ChipTips@ChipCummings.com

110

Creating the Reports

The reports should not be long — 2 to 3 pages are typical, as most people do not have the time (or attention span) for a lengthy dissertation! Take one of your selected topics and write down at least 5 things about that subject that people want or need to know. As an example, let's use "Credit." Five things I might list under that would include: 1) What credit scores are and how they are generated; 2) There are 3 major reporting repositories, and the information can be different; 3) Bad credit can remain on a report for 7 years or longer in most states; 4) Negative credit does not preclude someone from getting a mortgage; and 5) How someone goes about getting a copy of their credit report.

Just keep asking yourself questions — the questions clients have been asking you for years! This should get the creative juices going, and prompt you to think of several issues to list in your report. The next step is to actually write the report itself. You MUST have a GREAT headline! For a free detailed 121-page report on how to create great headlines, send me an e-mail at headlines@ChipCummings.com and I will walk you through it. The headline is what sells the prospect into coming inside — the report won't get read without a great one. For the example above, I might use *"The 5 Things You Need To Know About Credit Reports BEFORE Applying For A Loan" or "5 Credit Secrets Everyone Needs To Know."*

Next we need to look at the flow of the report itself. Start with a good solid (interest-generating) opening paragraph that will set the stage for the information you are about to share. Talk about each item on your list, and then sum it up with a call to action such as contacting you for more information. Make sure you include your phone, e-mail, website and physical address. Don't make this difficult or painful, just keep it simple and basic. You want to cover the topic completely, but invite them to contact you (as the expert) for more detailed explanation.

For a FREE 7-day course on "7 Steps To Building A Successful Marketing Plan," send an e-mail to ChipTips@ChipCummings.com

111

To create the second type of report — an affiliate partner report, the process is the same except you tap into the experience of other professionals. I might call a property appraiser and interview them for an hour on what goes into composing an appraisal, the differences for income vs. owner-occupied properties, and the 7 most common questions he gets from clients. If you are in the insurance industry, it would be interesting to talk to a claims adjuster, underwriter, or a fraud specialist.

Take the notes from your interview, and put them into an organized easy-to-read format, then ask the person whom you interviewed to review the report. Put their name on it as the expert resource, along with your name and your contact information for follow-up! Then allow the affiliate expert to share the report with *their* clients to create what is known as a "viral effect." In the mortgage lending world, this can be done with real estate agents, insurance reps, title companies, surveyors, CPA's, attorneys, financial planners, builders, interior designers, landscape architects, or moving companies — and that's just a short list!

Once the report is finished, ask a spouse, friend, relative or some one who is NOT in any way affiliated with the industry to read the report. The average 18-yr. old needs to be able to easily understand and comprehend the information in the report. Ask them what they learned and what parts were confusing or if certain areas of the report left them with questions. Then rewrite those sections. Only then will you be ready to share the report with the hungry public!

Sharing Your "Value"

Once you've created the reports, now comes the fun part — integrating the technology for instant automatic delivery. You need to share this new report with lots of interested people, so begin by printing, scanning or saving the report in a "PDF"

For a FREE 7-day course on "7 Steps To Building A Successful Marketing Plan," send an e-mail to ChipTips@ChipCummings.com

112

computer file format (if you are unfamiliar with PDF formatted documents, visit www.Adobe.com for more information). This allows anyone to easily open it from an e-mail attachment, and is a universally used format.

Statistics from Google, the largest Internet search engine, indicate that they receive over 200 million search requests per DAY, and estimates indicate they only account for approximately 41% of the total searches done! There are thousands of people in your immediate area looking for your expert information. However, from a marketing perspective, you want to capture the name and e-mail address of everyone who wants a copy of your report.

DO NOT just post the free report as a link on your website (or the affiliate partner's site). Remember, we are trying to create an "ethical bribe" where we *trade* value for name and e-mail address. If you just give them the report, you have no mechanism for follow-ups. Instead, use a simple web form capture (name and e-mail) next to your report headline that sends them to an autoresponder system (Chapter 8) and automatically adds them to your database to allow you to do additional follow-up marketing. You can also have cross-links from your affiliate partner's website to your free report web form, or have them simply send you an e-mail similar to what I asked you to do above!

As a final bonus, offer the report to the affiliate partner to use with *their* prospects or customers! Make it "hands-off" for them by providing a sample e-mail they can send to their client database, or as a part of their marketing program. This not only adds value for them (with no more than 1 hour of their time invested!), but also increases your reputation for providing expert resources in the marketplace. By controlling the distribution of the report, their marketing efforts will build your database and prospect list as well!

For a FREE 7-day course on "7 Steps To Building A Successful Marketing Plan," send an e-mail to ChipTips@ChipCummings.com

113

Once this report and delivery system is set up, it should run hands-free, and allow you to handle a steady flow (or huge onslaught!) of prospects, and create substantial personal "Chip Value" in the marketplace for years to come!

Remember, make these reports simple and straight forward (2-4 pages) and always include an invitation for them to contact you for more detailed information. Then, advertise that they can get these free reports both online (through search engine placement) and offline (through publications, your printed materials, networking groups, etc.)

Make sure your website address is on all your physical materials including your business card, brochures, and shop signage. Even your car can advertise your business and your website. Get a magnetic sign for your car with your website address prominently displayed, and/or get a plastic sticker for the inside of your rear window.

I have also used targeted direct mail, toll-free numbers, TV and radio, e-zines, affiliate promos, and many other mediums to attract *"suspects"* to a particular website. The method I choose varies depending on which target I'm after and what I want them to do. The key is to drive targeted suspects into the website where I can then move into phase 2 — conversion.

Converting traffic

A lot of website traffic, even targeted traffic, doesn't mean anything unless you have an easy way to **convert** them into prospects. Of the suspects that visit your site or web page, some will look and leave, but the ones that want the information you've promised will become prospects. They will give their name and e-mail address to receive the promised report containing information they want. You should automatically feed this e-mail

For a FREE 7-day course on "7 Steps To Building A Successful Marketing Plan," send an e-mail to ChipTips@ChipCummings.com

114

information into an autoresponder sequencer that instantly sends them the report and sets them up to receive similar informational reports at least seven times over the next few months. Autoresponders will be covered in greater detail in Chapter 8.

Don't clutter up your website homepage with lots of different offers and reports. If you are catering to different markets, get a separate website domain name and web page for each. Domain names are SO inexpensive, that I will often purchase different ones for each type of marketing strategy — just to track the responses! The point is that you want to be perceived as the expert with important quality information that they NEED to have. Don't "water down" your approach by having multiple offers on the same page.

You must then make the information they were drawn there to find easy to locate, identify and retrieve. Don't make them click four times to get the information while you inundate them with other offers-they don't care! One click only, or you will lose them.

Even though I have shown you how you can completely automate this process through technology applications, I truly believe that you must find a way to create a "personal" relationship with the prospect. Don't "hide" behind the technology and expect it to work miracles by itself. But, what technology does provide is a way to filter large amounts of qualified traffic down to serious leads while you sleep! It's what I call "sleep-working"! You still have to build trust, not hype, through the reports and autoresponders. Remember, people only do business with people they trust, and they only trust people they like. They cannot learn to like you from one visit to a website!

You can create a more "personal" relationship with a prospect through a series of personalized e-mails that are non-threatening (from a sales standpoint) and provide them with solid relevant

For a FREE 7-day course on "7 Steps To Building A Successful Marketing Plan," send an e-mail to ChipTips@ChipCummings.com

115

information. After a series of 7 to 10 contacts, they become much more connected to you, and then turn into warm leads!

Sometimes it works so well, that I have had new clients call me out of the blue like they were my best friend thanking me for just sending them that quick little e-mail update with some type of information, even though I've never spoken to them before. It's just because they have received specific personalized e-mails from me on a regular basis. Consistency is key to developing the relationship.

Getting Found

They best system in the world doesn't mean a dime in your pocket if nobody knows you're there! There are many different strategies you can adopt to make it easier for prospects to find your website. Here, I'll cover five important methods: search engines, keywords, Overture, Google AdWords, and Froogle.

Search engines

There are three extremely large search engines in the country, and dozens of smaller ones. The first search engine to hit the scene was Yahoo®. The current king of the search engine industry is Google®, but recently, MSN (and even Amazon!) added their own. These three along with a multitude of smaller ones search millions and millions of websites every day to find and categorize information that people are seeking. Similar to a huge "Yellow Pages" directory, when somebody types words or phrases that they are interested in, the search engine's job is to define and refine their criteria and automatically list websites or web pages that match the search criteria, then connect you to the right page. To give you an idea of the size of these directories, MSN currently touts listings of over 15 BILLION web pages!

For a FREE 7-day course on "7 Steps To Building A Successful Marketing Plan," send an e-mail to ChipTips@ChipCummings.com

116

If you've never searched the Web before, I encourage you to try this experiment when you finish reading: Go to any search engine (Google, Yahoo, Alta Vista, Jeeves, etc.) and type in your name. For example, if my customers are looking for me, they will type in "Chip Cummings", and hit search. While I'm not the famous Chip Cummings, the baseball player, if someone's looking for me, they can find me in dozens of spots. If somebody doesn't know my name, but they've heard of one of my companies, such as Northwind, they could search for that and find it. I'm all over the place, be it my business or personal websites, so people are able to find me from anywhere in the world. This didn't happen by accident, it takes some planning and knowledge of how the system works. If any of your prospects or customers click the search button after typing your name, they better find you!

If the domain name were the only ingredient for successful searches, the process would be simple. Unfortunately, there are a few more things that have to go into the mix to insure you get a top-ten billing. You have to be patient. The search engine companies use programs called "spiders" and "robots" that search and crawl through websites to feed the search engines, so obtaining numerous listings may take some time.

"Spiders" are search engine programs which go to websites and search for all attached web pages and documents, and through links they then find other websites and pages. "Robots" pick up where the spiders leave off, searching for certain types of information on a specific web page in order to categorize it and place it in the directories correctly. "Robots" look for keywords, phrases, links, pictures, and other related content to help judge the importance or relevancy to match consumer search inquiries.

When it comes to search engine position placement, there are ways you can increase the odds in your favor. In training and

For a FREE 7-day course on "7 Steps To Building A Successful Marketing Plan," send an e-mail to ChipTips@ChipCummings.com

117

consulting on technology marketing strategies with companies across the country, we've identified many of the "key ingredients" to making sure you get a top billing when it comes to the Internet search engines (and they all work a little differently). Search engines like to provide consumers with content — relevant content. So here are four simple things you can do to improve your position within the search engine directories:

1. Make sure that your company name (or personal name) is located in the title of your web page so search engines can find it! This is the line that appears in the top title bar section when you view a web page. For example, your web page source code (HTML) should contain something like the following line — <TITLE> ABC Financial — Conventional and FHA Residential Mortgage Loans Throughout Michigan </TITLE>.

2. Have a separate web page off of your main website that is specific to you as a business owner. Use your name in the TITLE header description (as described above), replacing the company name with your name.

3. Create *meta tags* for your "page description" and "keywords" that the search engines will match up with your name, title, and products or services. Include the specific keywords in each meta tag. Here's an example of a meta tag included in HTML source code:

   <meta name="Description" content="Experienced mortgage professionals providing residential mortgage loans throughout Michigan, including conventional and FHA lending.">

   <meta name="keywords" content="mortgage loans, ABC Financial, Michigan loans, Chip Cummings, Michigan conventional mortgage, residential financing, Michigan FHA

For a FREE 7-day course on "7 Steps To Building A Successful Marketing Plan," send an e-mail to ChipTips@ChipCummings.com

118

loans,…">, as well as other appropriate keywords and phrases. I will discuss how to find the actual keywords in a minute.

4. The rules for "keywords" are pretty simple-don't repeat any keyword in the meta keywords tag more than three times, and don't repeat any one keyword right after each other. This appears like "SPAM" to the search engine.

5. Make sure to use your company name and your own name several times (at least 5-7) within the body text of your web pages. The search engines will check to see if your keywords and phrases are used as part of the content, and will rank the value your information (and your listing) much higher. Don't overuse this strategy though, as keyword "jamming" through repetitive unnecessary use will count against you.

Selecting keywords

The Holy Grail of web search placement is to show up within the first few listings on the first page of the search results. To achieve one of these top positions, your website will have to contain many keywords, and relevant content. In order to find you, what are the most common words or phrases that your clients would use? These words should be included in your website's headings, metatags, and the body of your text. You will have to decide if it's worth your time and money to learn all these techniques yourself or if you should hire a company that specializes in search engine placement. Even if you decide to hire it out, you should understand the basics of what to look for on your site. Remember, even if you use a "template" site, YOU need to control the storefront — the main index homepage.

So, how do you research keywords? If you can find out where on the Internet your target market is "hanging out," you can then

For a FREE 7-day course on "7 Steps To Building A Successful Marketing Plan," send an e-mail to ChipTips@ChipCummings.com

119

target this audience with the appropriate keywords. The best way to do this is by finding out the exact words and phrases that people are searching for on the major search engines. There are three good free resources that provide this kind of research. The first is the Yahoo! Overture Search Term Suggestion Tool located at the following web address:

http://www.inventory.overture.com

When you reach this site, click on "Search Term Selection Tool." When you type a core keyword in the tool, it displays all related keywords searched over the past month as well as the number of people who *actually* searched for that specific term! This will give you a good idea of the popularity of certain words and phrases, and will probably show you a few surprises as well. But remember, this is only for searches conducted on the Overture system (which is owned by Yahoo!) To get an idea of the number of overall searches on different search engines, take that number and multiply by 8. That will give you a rough idea of the search traffic for that particular search term.

Another similar free tool is Google's Keyword Search Tool, which is a part of the Google AdWords service. You can find it at:

https://adwords.google.com/select/keywordtoolexternal

Type in one keyword such as "first-time homebuyer" or "auto insurance quotes", and the results will show you similar keyword search terms used by interested customers. While it doesn't show the actual number of searches, it will provide a pretty lengthy list of comparative search terms.

Another tool that I use is a free software program from Softnik Technologies, called Good Keywords. This software can search multiple search engines, and will provide the search counts as well — even in real time! You can find this helpful tool at www.GoodKeywords.com.

For a FREE 7-day course on "7 Steps To Building A Successful Marketing Plan," send an e-mail to ChipTips@ChipCummings.com

120

With these tools, you know exactly what words and phrases your suspects were searching for over the past month. You can use this information to create a list of potential keywords that you can use for your own website. I will discuss some additional features of Overture and Google AdWords in more detail later in this chapter.

Submitting to search engines

Once you complete your web pages, you have to submit them to the various search engines so browsers can find the information on your products and/or services. There are specific guidelines and tips for website submissions, and there are several companies out there that can assist you with this function, including Yahoo! and MSN. But you don't need to spend any money to get your website listed. You do have to spend a little time, but the rewards are well worth it.

The major search engines to which you should submit your site include Google, Yahoo!, MSN and DMOZ. From these, all the other search engines will eventually find your website links. It is important to make sure your site is completed and ready BEFORE you submit it! Do not submit a site that is still "under construction."

You can register your website with the main search engines in two ways. You can either manually submit your registration to each search engine or you can use one of several registration services to do the job for you. Registration services such as Microsoft's Submit-It.com let you enter basic information about your site once and then, for a fee, they submit your information to various search engines.

Whether you register once with a registration service or with the different search engines individually, be prepared to provide some basic information about your site. Although the required

For a FREE 7-day course on "7 Steps To Building A Successful Marketing Plan," send an e-mail to ChipTips@ChipCummings.com

121

registration information varies with different search engines and registration services, here is a list of common information that they might require:

+ Your Website's URL address (main domain name only).

+ A list of keywords that describe your Website.

+ A 35-to-50-word description of your Website.

+ The name, e-mail address, and phone number of a contact person.

Make sure that you only submit your main website index page! Do not submit each individual page, because this will only waste time and possibly get you banned from the search engine. Also, do not use "cloaking" tricks (misleading domain names that redirect to another site), invisible text or links, link farms, home page pop-ups, or attempts to "spam" your keywords into the text. The search engines know how to spot these tricks and will respond by banning your site from inclusion.

When you submit your website to the search engine (see listing at the end of this Chapter), it will then be added to their "spider" search for inclusion in their listings. Be patient! As a general rule, search engine spiders will only visit your site once every 3-6 weeks. All searches are done automatically, with the exception of the DMOZ project. The Open Directory Project (www.dmoz.org) is a submission site that reviews each submission through a human "category editor." This specialist will visit your site, and if approved, add it to the appropriate directory categories. Inclusion in this search engine is not automatic, and can be a slow process. It also has come under some fire, since "personal bias" can play a factor over whether or not you get listed.

For a FREE 7-day course on "7 Steps To Building A Successful Marketing Plan," send an e-mail to ChipTips@ChipCummings.com

122

Getting your website listed on a search engine isn't enough. Out of all the results that come up for a search, people will generally look at only the first 7-10 entries on the list. Work to make sure that when your customer is surfing, searching, and looking, that you are near the top of that list. Otherwise, they might just click on your competitor's link!

While the actual formulas that search engines use to compile their listings are closely guarded secrets, use some common sense. People are searching for specific information, so the listings will reflect the quality of appropriate content and relevant keywords, and the quality of the cross-links contained in and out of the site. Search engines also like to see "fresh information." Make sure that you change something on your website at least once every 6 to 8 weeks. This will increase your ranking, because search engines deem newer updated information as more relevant during searches. There are some advanced strategies for providing fresh information automatically, including RSS feeds, live data links, and XML feeds — but that's another story!

Tracking your position

It is equally important to track the overall rating of your website, including how many people are visiting you! How do I know that www.MSN.com is the number two most visited website? There is a special free toolbar that you can obtain that will provide you with a wealth of information about website rankings and popularity. If you visit the Alexa website (Alexa.com), you can search on any domain name or URL and get its Internet ranking. Owned by Amazon, Alexa is itself a search engine and website ranking service.

Alexa also provides a free toolbar that you can add to your browser. This toolbar provides all kinds of useful information

For a FREE 7-day course on "7 Steps To Building A Successful Marketing Plan," send an e-mail to ChipTips@ChipCummings.com

123

about websites on the Internet. This is one of the best secrets when you're doing website research for your websites or any others. When you download and use this tool, it tells you the page ranking for any site you visit. It also shows you all the information about who owns that site, "who goes there," how many links are hooked to the website, other related sites that people visit, as well as traffic statistics. Make sure to download this toolbar!

Overture

Overture is a wholly owned subsidiary of Yahoo!, Inc. They were one of the first companies to offer "pay-per-click" search result placement. This is where you can actually place your site in the list for certain keywords and then pay a small fee if and when someone actually clicks on your link. In addition to the above mentioned free Search Term Selection Tool, Overture offers other services including the following:

Precision Match™: Overture displays your website as a sponsored link in the search results on leading sites like Yahoo, MSN, and AltaVista. When you enroll, you select keywords that relate to your website and when users enter those keywords, your website appears in search results on Overture's partner sites (including Yahoo!, Alta Vista, MSN and others). You pay a small fee ($.05 up) each time a person clicks on the link to your site. You manage your costs by setting the price you are willing to pay per click, and how much you want to pay per day. Similar to an auction, the more you decide to pay per click, the higher your website links appear within the search results.

Local Match™: This service is very similar to Precision Match, except that it helps you precisely target customers in

For a FREE 7-day course on "7 Steps To Building A Successful Marketing Plan," send an e-mail to ChipTips@ChipCummings.com

124

your neighborhood who search for local products and services. This enables you to only reach people within a particular state, city or region.

Content Match™: This service uses the same pay-per-click system to display your website listing inside resource boxes positioned next to articles, product reviews, and other information on sites like CNN.com, ESPN.com, Yahoo!, and MSN.com.

Site Match™: This program compliments the Precision Match program. It optimizes your website link for inclusion in the main body of the search results page. This makes your link look like a regular part of the search results rather than a sponsored link (i.e. advertisement).

Google AdWords

Similar to Overture, Google has a pay-per-click website advertising option called AdWords. Based upon personal experience, I have had better results with this program than any of the others out there. With the AdWords program, you create a sponsored link that appears in a box, positioned to the right of the main body of search results, on a topic-appropriate Google search-results page.

How much do you pay for each click? With Google, that depends on you. After a $5 activation fee, you set how much you are willing to pay per click and per day. You do not get to view and "auction" your placement bid like Overture, but you can choose a maximum cost-per-click (CPC) from $0.05 to $50 and set a daily budget as low as 5 cents or go as high as you want. There is no minimum monthly charge and you only pay for people who actually click through to your site.

As for ad placement, Google AdWords does not rank ads

For a FREE 7-day course on "7 Steps To Building A Successful Marketing Plan," send an e-mail to ChipTips@ChipCummings.com

125

solely on cost. There is no way to "reserve" the top placement in the AdWords program. Ad placement is based on a combination of your maximum CPC and click-through rate (CTR). This means that if you earn a higher CTR, you are rewarded with a lower actual CPC and a higher position.

Adwords also allows you to regionalize your placements, using different countries, states and/or cities to refine your target market. Their system includes useful reports and tracking data, and allows you to have separate URL links for individual keywords if desired! You can research Google AdWords by visiting www.AdWords.Google.com.

Froogle

Froogle is another Google service that helps people find information about products for sale online. Because it focuses entirely on product searches, Froogle applies the power of Google's search technology to the very specific task of locating online stores that sell the item you want. Froogle is most useful if you operate an online store that sells products. Unlike other online shopping sites, Froogle is completely free. There is no spending account to set up and maintain and no cost-per-click.

How do you get in Froogle? Actually, if you operate an online store, Google might already have you indexed in Froogle since Google crawls billions of web pages every month looking for sites to add. However, the best way to be included in Froogle is to submit what they call a "data feed." To send them a data feed, you first submit some basic information about your store. After they verify that your store conforms to their program policies, you can follow their data feed instructions to have your products included in Froogle.

For a FREE 7-day course on "7 Steps To Building A Successful Marketing Plan," send an e-mail to ChipTips@ChipCummings.com

126

AdSense

Another one of Google's programs designed to allow you to make money off of their PPC program is AdSense. This works in the reverse fashion of the AdWords structure, in that it allows you to place keyword relevant search PPC ads from others on your website. Each time someone clicks on one of these ads through your site, you get a small commission. This works well for product sites with listing for complimentary products or services. For more info, visit www.AdSense.Google.com.

Making it Work-An Example

Here is a scenario of how you might apply these techniques to your website using a mortgage business as an example:

1. First, you find the keywords your clients are using. To do that, you visit the Overture keyword search tool at http://www.content.overture.com/d/USm/ac/index.jhtml. After you select "Search Term Selection Tool" you type in one keyword such as "first-time homebuyer," and the results will show you similar keyword search terms used by interested customers, as well as the number of searches done for the previous month.

    In one such experiment, I found that 36,591 people used the term "first time homebuyer." More importantly, 601 people also searched specifically for "Florida first-time homebuyer." Keep in mind that this is only the results from one search engine. You can extrapolate (using search engine market percentages) that as many as 6200 specific searches were done by first-time homebuyers in Florida. Print out or make a list of the most popular keyword search terms for your target market.

For a FREE 7-day course on "7 Steps To Building A Successful Marketing Plan," send an e-mail to ChipTips@ChipCummings.com

127

2. On the main Overture page, select "View Bids Tool" to see what it would cost you to market to that specific group. For the Florida example, you would type "Florida first-time homebuyer."

My sample results indicate that you could place a mini-ad link in the third position for $0.96 per click! Personally, I would gladly pay 96 cents for a chance to capture specific first-time homebuyers in Florida looking for information. These are very warm leads! The key is to avoid bidding for the top 1-2 spots or "general" keyword terms. It is too expensive for the response you'll get, and you will get better results (better qualified suspects) with more specific terms (and they will cost less).

3. Next, create an ad that offers information. The ad should have a strong headline, such as "For a free e-book on creating headlines, send a blank e-mail to headlines@ChipCummings.com", and be written to include the benefits to the prospect. For example, sticking with our mortgage scenario, you could offer a free informational report, payment calculator, pre-qualification checklist, or something similar. For products, concentrate on the solution that it offers. Feed the link to an autoresponder system that allows you to deliver the information automatically, and follow up with them in a "soft sell" environment. Chapter 8 will cover autoresponders in more detail.

4. Now that you have researched the specific keywords that are being searched for by your target market, you need to take those keywords and make sure they are being used in your website pages. Then, create a description tag for your web page that uses combinations of those words. For example,

For a FREE 7-day course on "7 Steps To Building A Successful Marketing Plan," send an e-mail to ChipTips@ChipCummings.com

128

you could use the following phrases in the body content: "We specialize in providing financing to first-time homebuyers in Florida" or "We know that first-time homebuyers have lots of questions about how to get into that first home, so we have a team of six loan officers located right in our Miami, Florida office dedicated to helping just first-time homebuyers!"

The description tag for your website page might read "Helping first-time homebuyers in Florida achieve their dream of owning a home with little or no money and no credit. Receive our FREE report "Becoming A First-time Homebuyer in Florida." You should also use a combination of the keywords in your website headline and/or sub-headline as well.

5. Once you have the structure in place, the next step is to let the world know how to find you. The search engine robots will eventually find all your keywords and keyword phrases, which will rank your website higher for those keyword searches. To make it happen faster, go to http://www.Google.com/addurl.html and type in your main website page (i.e. http://www.ABCMortgage.com). Do NOT submit all of your web pages-that will only work against you. Your results will be better if you let the spider crawler find those pages on its own. Why Google? Because they are the 1000-pound gorilla of the Internet, and control the largest percentage of the searches done around the world. Other smaller search engines will eventually find you through Google as well.

6. Submit the same information to at least Yahoo!, MSN and the DMOZ sites.

For a FREE 7-day course on "7 Steps To Building A Successful Marketing Plan," send an e-mail to ChipTips@ChipCummings.com

129

Internet search engine sites

As of time of publication, here is a list of search engine sites where you can register your website (subject to change):

Google
http://www.Google.com/addurl.html

MSN
http://beta.search.msn.com/docs/submit.aspx

Yahoo!
http://search.yahoo.com/info/submit.html

DMOZ — *(DMOZ also provides search data to other major search engines)*
http://dmoz.com/add.html

Ask Jeeves
https://sitesubmit.ask.com/Main/login.jsp

Submit It
http://www.submit-it.com

Look Smart
http://www.looksmart.com/r?page=/SearchSolutions/zeal_grub/zeal_grub.html

Mamma — *Mamma is another pay-per-click service.*
http://www.MammaMediaSolutions.com/advertisers/ppc/index.html

Dogpile
https://secure.ah-ha.com/guaranteed_inclusion/teaser.aspx?network=dogpile

For a FREE 7-day course on "7 Steps To Building A Successful Marketing Plan," send an e-mail to ChipTips@ChipCummings.com

130

AOL
http://search.aol.com/aolcom/add.jsp

iWon
http://www.iWon.com

Searchre
http://www.searchfeed.com/rd/index.jsp

Yahoo! Overture — *Overture is a pay-per-click service.*
http://www.overture.com

Keyword Search Tool
http://www.inventory.overture.com

Lycos
http://insite.lycos.com/

Excite
https://secure.ah-ha.com/guaranteed_inclusion/teaser.aspx

Webcrawler
http://www.webcrawler.com

HotBot
http://www.HotBot.com

For a FREE 7-day course on "7 Steps To Building A Successful Marketing Plan," send an e-mail to ChipTips@ChipCummings.com

131

CHIP TIPS:

Here are your "personal road signs" from this Chapter:

1. Your customers move through an evolutionary process that starts with suspects representing your target audience. Your goal is to move them from Suspects to Prospects and eventually to Evangelists.

2. Your website is your central marketing tool. Its only purpose is to capture a name and e-mail address. To do this, you must target traffic on the Internet and drive it to your website and convert visitors to prospects.

3. Search engine placement is the life blood of your website. Research appropriate keywords using Overture's Search Term Suggestion Tool or Google's Keyword Search Tool. Then, submit the index page of your website to Google, Yahoo, and DMOZ at a minimum.

4. Use Overture and Google AdWords to get optimum ad placement for your website on search results pages. When you use pay-per-click advertising, try to get the third or fourth position; don't purchase the first or second position- it's too expensive and the third and fourth ads are better positioned near the center of the page.

5. If you sell physical products, get your website listed with Froogle, a free product search engine maintained by Google.

For a FREE 7-day course on "7 Steps To Building A Successful Marketing Plan," send an e-mail to ChipTips@ChipCummings.com

132

Chapter 8

Reaching 20,000 People While You Sleep

"Things may come to those who wait, but only the things left by those who hustle."

Abraham Lincoln

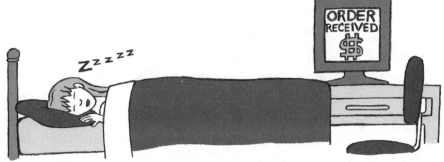

"**S**leep-working" is the ability to automate your system to the point that it generates quality traffic, converting suspects into prospects, and generating a steady stream of customers — while you sleep!

A recent study conducted by Sales and Marketing International concluded that 81% of all major sales are conducted after the fifth contact! Many other studies support that fact, stressing that you need to "touch" a prospect 6-7 times before they will make a buying decision. That means you will have to talk to prospects more than once; maybe two or three times before they even remember who you are!

For a FREE 7-day course on "7 Steps To Building A Successful Marketing Plan," send an e-mail to ChipTips@ChipCummings.com

133

That's where the autoresponder approach comes in. In my overall technology marketing strategy, the website is the central focus. I drive people there for information, "Chip Value" items, applications, questions, qualifying, rates, events, newsletters, etc., with the intent of sorting Suspects into Prospects. My main goal for the qualified Prospects is to at least capture a name and e-mail address through the Ethical Bribe technique. From there, I can systematically follow up through electronic means. This way, I can spend personal time on the serious prospects.

As we continue the "Rule of Reach" concept in this chapter, we'll look at specific ways autoresponders can help you automatically follow up on Prospects to convert them into leads.

Autoresponder Basics

If you've been fairly active on the Internet at all, odds are you have probably already been the subject of an autoresponder! E-mail autoresponders are pre-written messages set up to instantly and automatically respond to an order, e-mail inquiry, or message. If you have ever ordered anything on-line and gotten an instant confirmation, receipt, or "thank you" e-mail back, the message was probably generated by an autoresponder. The catch is, few people have realized how to use this technology effectively for marketing!

Until a few years ago, you could only send out one autoresponder message at a time. Now it's possible to program a whole series of messages to be delivered automatically at different intervals. Also, you can customize the autoresponder message with personal information such as the recipients' first name or other collected data.

For example, when a Prospect submits an inquiry, message #1 might go out immediately. Then message #2 goes out 2 days

For a FREE 7-day course on "7 Steps To Building A Successful Marketing Plan," send an e-mail to ChipTips@ChipCummings.com

134

later, followed by message #3 on the 6th day, message #4 on the 10th day, and so on. The best part is that you can pre-program this messaging system to automatically start the sequence when a customer sends an e-mail or fills out an online form. That means that you set the system up once and it will keep on working over and over again without you having to touch it! You can literally reach 20,000 people while you sleep!

Setting Up the System

To set up this type of system, you need help from e-mail marketing specialists. I use several companies, but one of the best and most versatile is available at SimpleAutoresponders.com. On a monthly basis, the system should only run you about $19.95 per month, or $179 per year. The cost is reasonable, and the investment is pennies based upon the results. Visit the site and sign up for their "test-drive." They also have instructional videos to get you started. There are several other companies who specialize in this form of marketing, including Autoresponders.com, autobots.net, and automailer.com to name just a few.

Make sure the system you use allows for multiple lists, unlimited numbers of subscribers and messages, reporting functions, list import and export features, CAN-SPAM Act compliance, opt-in tracking, simple unsubscribe functions, and are extremely reputable. Without your knowledge, they could be banned from some ISP's and your messages would be deleted before they ever got a chance to be delivered! Quality systems will also provide a SPAM analyzer feature that helps you check your autoresponder messages prior to sending them out. Take your time to select the company you work with, because it's a LOT of work to switch later on!

Another interesting site is autoresponder-review.com. This site strives to provide relevant and useful comparisons of auto

For a FREE 7-day course on "7 Steps To Building A Successful Marketing Plan," send an e-mail to ChipTips@ChipCummings.com

135

responders. In each review they discuss the pros and cons of the service and provide pricing information. They also provide articles on maximizing results from auto responders.

Creating the Message

After you have chosen the autoresponder system you want to use, and become familiar with its features, you're ready to create the autoresponder message series. To build a successful autoresponder series, you need to create an attention grabbing headline, write great message copy, and craft a message that avoids spam filters.

Writing an attention grabbing headline

The most important ingredient of any autoresponder message is the subject headline! Without an attention grabbing subject line, your message will never get past the delete button!

You need to have a subject headline that creates interest and forces them to open it! Keep the headline short, intriguing, and use a verb whenever possible. The best headlines use words like "Discover," "Create," "Learn," "Develop," "Act," "Find Out," or in the form of questions. Also, try to personalize the message by including their first name in subject line and in the body of the message itself. For a free report on creating headlines, send me an e-mail at Headlines@ChipCummings.com.

Writing the message copy

As for the body of the message, it is important that you format your e-mails to 65 characters per line or less. Everyone's e-mail programs are different, and you want to be sure they are able to read it easily without distraction. If you just type your message

For a FREE 7-day course on "7 Steps To Building A Successful Marketing Plan," send an e-mail to ChipTips@ChipCummings.com

136

in a word processor using automatic word-wrap, it may not flow correctly in your recipient's e-mail program, and could appear like this on their screen:

Dear Scott,

Thank you for

responding to our offer of a free report on

becoming

a first-time homebuyer....

When you use word wrap, the spacing may not follow the format you intended. Because the recipient's e-mail program may be different than yours, some lines and sentences of your message could include unintended breaks in the wording structure. This becomes distracting for the reader and takes away from your message. If you keep your lines to a 65 character width, you insure that they will be able to follow your message easily even with basic software programs.

The secret to making your lines 65 characters (or less), is to use a "hard return." That means you press the "Enter" key when you approach 65 spaces. Also, use a basic font that the recipient's computer can easily display. Fancy fonts may look nice, but not if the recipient doesn't have that exact same font. Use Arial, Times New Roman, or Courier for the best results.

Most autoresponder programs provide a feature to "automatically wrap" the lines at 65 characters for you. However, the easiest way to format your message is to use a word processor like Microsoft Word, and then save it in .TXT file format. I use a simple ruler at the top to guide me as to when I should insert a hard return:

————1————2————3————4————5————6——/

For a FREE 7-day course on "7 Steps To Building A Successful Marketing Plan," send an e-mail to ChipTips@ChipCummings.com

137

You also want to use an autoresponder service that lets you customize the e-mail with the recipient's personal information. Usually you will only use basic information about the recipient such as first name, last name, and e-mail address. Often, I use their first name in the subject line and in the body of the message so they become more comfortable with the information and approach. It personalizes the e-mail message, so they feel that it was written specifically from me to them. Typically, you insert personalized information using placeholder text. For example, for the first name you might insert "<$firstname$>" and the autoresponder automatically inserts each person's first name from the information it captured when they opted-in to your system.

Avoiding SPAM filters

Tom Kulzer, CEO of aWeber Systems, a top autoresponder firm recently indicated that an estimated 1.7 Billion pieces of e-mail are automatically deleted each day on the AOL system alone — simply because they "looked" like SPAM. An estimated 20% of those were probably GOOD e-mails that were personally sent and should have gotten through! Since a computer is evaluating your e-mail, you must also avoid certain words in your message, or your e-mail will never get through! SPAM filters look for specific words and text patterns. If too many key words or phrases are present, your message will get deleted before the recipient even has a chance to see it!

Here are some ways to avoid SPAM filters:

✦ Avoid words such as "free," "hello," "no cost," "no obligation," "try it today," and other similar such triggers.

✦ Don't use excited language with lots of exclamation points (!) and/or capital letters.

For a FREE 7-day course on "7 Steps To Building A Successful Marketing Plan," send an e-mail to ChipTips@ChipCummings.com

138

✦ Spell check your message and use appropriate grammar.

✦ Avoid using RED text or too many web links in the message.

✦ If you must use words like FREE, then break it up in the text, such as F.R.E.E. or FRE E.

✦ Avoid all declarations such as "THIS IS NOT SPAM." Don't even use the word SPAM in your messages. Let the recipient decide whether it's SPAM or not.

Timing Your Messages

When planning your autoresponder system, you have to answer two key questions: how many and how often? It's a balancing act. You want to send enough messages to keep them engaged, but not so many that you irritate them. You want to time the messages far enough apart so as not to overwhelm them, but not so far apart that they forget why they requested the information from you in the first place!

For a typical series, I use 7 individual messages spread out over an initial 6 to 8 week period, with additional follow-up options and links. In other series, I use as many as 40 messages and as few as 5, but I recommend a minimum of 7 for the best response. These autoresponder e-mails contain answers to their most frequent questions, and provide additional reports and resources. With the continuous personal communication and valuable information they receive, almost all serious shoppers eventually end up on my customer list. At worst, they become educated consumers!

How do you know the correct balance? Easy — listen to the people that opt-in to the list! It's obvious that you don't want to send 5 messages at once, or several within just a few days. If

For a FREE 7-day course on "7 Steps To Building A Successful Marketing Plan," send an e-mail to ChipTips@ChipCummings.com

139

people are "opting out" of the list, it means one of two things — they are not getting the information they want, or they are annoyed by the frequency of the messages. Likewise, if they are opting out after the fourth message, then you have a problem with either timing or content in message three.

One successful strategy you can employ is to package your autoresponder as a multi-part series of reports or online lessons for a course. Just make sure you create information that is useful, interesting, and designed to trigger a response. For example, here is a series of reports I offer to first-time home buyers which are delivered over a period of about 60 days:

1. *Getting Prepared For Homeownership — What You Need To Know!*

2. *How Much House and How Much Payment Can I Afford?*

3. *What They Don't Want You To Know About Interest Rates!*

4. *What's My Score and Other Credit Reporting Mysteries!*

5. *Getting Into A Home For Little or NO Down Payment!*

6. *Making Sense Out Of Mortgage Programs — What's For ME?*

7. *The Search Is On — Real Estate Agent or FSBO?*

As you see, each of these reports address an individual topic so as not to overload the recipient too quickly with too much information at one time. The reports are also not too lengthy-usually just a page or two. Each report is designed to get them to call me and consult with them for professional advice and follow-up. If the report is too lengthy, they will just skim over it, or worse yet, not read it at all.

For a FREE 7-day course on "7 Steps To Building A Successful Marketing Plan," send an e-mail to ChipTips@ChipCummings.com

140

A Sample Message Series

To illustrate an example of a message series, I'll demonstrate a "first-time homebuyer" series, in which I will use 7 sequential messages sent to the customer over a period of about 1 month. This sample series was designed to capture specific new customers, who are very unfamiliar with the real estate buying process, but could be used for ANY type of business or service. Again, as a general rule I keep the messages fairly short, so the recipient can read them quickly. This series also assumes that the customer has "opted-in" or responded to an offer from an advertisement, website offer, or other capture method.

Here are the messages I might use:

Message #1

Sent — Immediately
Subject Line: Welcome <$firstname$>! — Getting Prepared For Homeownership

Dear <$firstname$>,

Thank you for your inquiry about the basics of buying a home. Attached is the report that I promised you, entitled "Getting Prepared For Home Ownership." This report will explain many of the basics in understanding what goes into looking for, selecting, and purchasing a home.

Please review the attached report at your convenience, and feel free to call me with any questions you might have. You are under no obligation, and real estate agents or any sales rep will call you.

You see <$firstname$>, buying a home is a big decision, and we want to be sure you understand the process and are aware

For a FREE 7-day course on "7 Steps To Building A Successful Marketing Plan," send an e-mail to ChipTips@ChipCummings.com

141

of the right questions to ask BEFORE you ever talk to
anyone. As a result of my personally working with hundreds
of new homebuyers just like you, I know that you
have many questions. For your convenience, I'll forward
you another report in a few days which explains a bit
about interest rates, and how they affect you and how much
you can afford.

In the meantime <$firstname$>, if you have any questions about
the report or the home buying process in general, please
feel free to call me at (xxx) xxx-xxxx. Thanks again for
your interest, and I wish you the best —

Sincerely,

Chip Cummings, CMC
ABC Financial Corporation

Message #2

Sent — 2 days later
Subject Line: <$firstname$>, how much house can you afford?

<$firstname$> —

Hi! Hope you had a chance to look at the report I sent you
a few days ago. As you can see, there is a lot that goes
into the process, and the first place to start is with the
financing.

After working with thousands of people over the past 18
years, I know one of the most basic questions you must
have is — How much house can I actually afford?

For a FREE 7-day course on "7 Steps To Building A Successful Marketing Plan," send an e-mail to ChipTips@ChipCummings.com

142

I have attached a quick report for you that explains the
basics of qualifying, and what formulas lenders typically
use to calculate payments and possible loan amounts.
There are several programs that allow you to get into a
new home with very little or even no money down! This
report will illustrate the basics of what money might be
needed for the purchase of a home, and some of the options
for down payments.

Take a look at the report <$firstname$>, and let me know if you
have any questions. Another report that I have prepared
looks at interest rates and how they relate to qualifying.
I'll pass that one on to you in a few days.

Thanks again, and happy reading!

Sincerely,

Chip Cummings, CMC
ABC Financial Corp.

Message #3

Sent — 4 days later
Subject Line: <$firstname$> — here's The REAL Story on Interest Rates

Greetings <$firstname$>!

Interest rates are low, as everyone on the planet knows by now.
What you may not know, is that interest rates are only a part of
the equation!

For a FREE 7-day course on "7 Steps To Building A Successful Marketing Plan," send an e-mail to ChipTips@ChipCummings.com

143

Let me explain <$firstname$>.......

Yes, you can certainly save money on your payment with lower interest rates, but there are several other factors that influence the TRUE interest rate that you pay! Just because someone offers a 4.00% interest rate, doesn't mean that it all there is to the story.

<$firstname$>, there are hundreds of different mortgage programs out there, and all of them have different types of interest rate and cost structures attached to them. To help you sift through all the hype, I have prepared a short report for you called "The REAL Story on Interest Rates." It'll help you understand the relationship between rate and cost, and why they can vary — and that interest rate should NOT be the only thing you look at!

I have found that an educated homeowner is a happy homeowner, and want to be sure that all your questions are answered. If you are interested in talking about your specific qualifications and circumstances, please feel free to call me at (xxx) xxx-xxxx. I'll be glad to give you a half-hour of my time, with no obligation of course, to answer any questions you still might have.

Hope to talk to you soon —

-Chip Cummings

Message #4

Sent — 4 days later
Subject Line: <$firstname$>, Have you checked your credit history?

For a FREE 7-day course on "7 Steps To Building A Successful Marketing Plan," send an e-mail to ChipTips@ChipCummings.com

144

<$firstname$> —

Hope the report on interest rates helped you out. There's a
lot of misleading information in the marketplace, huh?

One thing I forgot to mention the other day, and that concerns
credit reports. Obviously credit plays an important part in
the overall equation as well. What many people don't
understand, is that your credit doesn't have to perfect
(who's is, right?) to get a new home!

In fact, there are many programs designed for people that
have a few "bumps" in their past, but that doesn't have to
be a problem.

Knowing that one of the first things you might want to look
at is your credit <$firstname$>, I have attached a sheet which
explains a little more about credit reports, and where
you can go if there are errors or to get copies (sometimes
they can cost a few bucks). Of course, I'll be glad to
run a credit report for you at no cost, and look over to
see if there are any items that would be of concern to a lender.

If you would like me to provide you with a complimentary
copy of your credit report, just give me a call at (xxx)
xxx-xxxx, and we can get one right away for you.

Take care <$firstname$>, and let me know if you need anything
else —

-Chip

For a FREE 7-day course on "7 Steps To Building A Successful Marketing Plan," send an e-mail to ChipTips@ChipCummings.com

145

Message #5

Sent — 5 days later
Subject Line: <$firstname$> — Interested in buying a home with little or no money?

<$firstname$> —

Hi, me again...... Just wanted to let you know about a
couple of special programs that are designed for first-time
homebuyers — specifically with little or no down payment
required!

Knowing that many first-time homebuyers don't have a lot
of extra cash to work with, I developed that attached
report as a quick guide on what options might be available.
Take a look at it <$firstname$>, and let me know if you have
any questions. As always, you can call me at (xxx) xxx-xxxx.

Look forward to talking to you soon —

-Chip

Message #6

Sent — 5 days later
Subject Line: <$firstname$>, let's look at possible financing options

Hi <$firstname$>!

I know I've loaded you down with a whole lot of info lately,
but hope you're finding it informative. The idea is to know
about all this financing stuff before you make the final
commitment on buying your new home.

For a FREE 7-day course on "7 Steps To Building A Successful Marketing Plan," send an e-mail to ChipTips@ChipCummings.com

146

In addition to the little to no-money down programs that I told
you about a few days ago, there are a few other programs
you might be interested, so I attached a quick report for
you <$firstname$>.

It's time we got you Pre-Approved for the loan, which as
you know we can get done in less than a day. I won't
don't charge you a dime, since I won't get paid anything
unless you find a house, AND I get you the money for it!

Look over the attached info, then give me a call <$firstname$> -
I'd love to go over it.

Talk soon —

-Chip

Message #7

Sent — 7 days later
Subject Line: <$firstname$>, how's the search going?

<$firstname$> —

Just wondered how the search was going.......

Many times, people ask me about the advantages of working
with a real estate agent, or trying to find a house on their own.

I don't know <$firstname$>, there are advantages to both! I've
enclosed another short report on working with agents and
also "For Sale By Owners" (who we affectionately call

For a FREE 7-day course on "7 Steps To Building A Successful Marketing Plan," send an e-mail to ChipTips@ChipCummings.com

147

FiSBO's!) which talks about the right questions to ask,
and the process of making an offer on a house.

Believe me <$firstname$>, I know what a scary step that can be!
It doesn't have to though, and you want to make sure it's
structured and presented in the best possible way for you.
Look over the info, and call me when you get a chance —
I have plenty of resources to assist you with every detail
of the hunt!

Happy hunting, and look forward to talking to you
soon <$firstname$> —

-Chip
(xxx) xxx-xxxx

As you can see, these messages get more informal and take on a personal tone as they progress. This makes the customer comfortable with me as a professional and as a "trusted friend." Usually I receive a call from the recipient within the first 3 to 4 messages, so make sure the later messages compliment any other conversations you might have had. Just keep them simple and give the recipient a reason to call you for more information. That way you have another opportunity to sell yourself.

Managing Your Database

Autoresponder series can be created for attracting new clients, communicating with current clients, and staying in touch with past clients-all automatically! As people sign up for your information via your web site, separate your autoresponder database into at least three groups: past, present, and future customers.

For a FREE 7-day course on "7 Steps To Building A Successful Marketing Plan," send an e-mail to ChipTips@ChipCummings.com

148

This has two advantages. First, this provides you a way to track the success of the message series individually within each group. Second, once someone moves from future customer to present customer or past customer, it is inappropriate to keep sending them messages intended for their old group. It also allows you to periodically send timely "broadcast" messages with different contexts to each list separately.

The better autoresponder systems provide a way to automatically remove someone from one list and assign them to another based on some action they take like ordering a product online, or requesting a certain report.

Seven Steps for Autoresponder Success

Here are seven steps you need to follow that help to create the maximum response and customer pull:

1. **Create an attention grabbing headline.** The subject line (headline) is crucial. Encourage the recipient to open the message by making it interesting and compelling. Keep it short, and where possible, use the recipients' first name in the message.

2. **Personalize the message.** Use their name in the body of the message. This can be automated from within the autoresponder service provider. If appropriate, use other database fields for the series, but don't overuse this feature or it comes across as "canned."

3. **Use "triggers" and a response mechanism.** Always include some type of free offer, benefit or reason to contact you for more (i.e. free credit report, financial physical, personal consultation, etc.). ALWAYS use a postscript (P.S.) at the end of the message and include the trigger. Statistics show

For a FREE 7-day course on "7 Steps To Building A Successful Marketing Plan," send an e-mail to ChipTips@ChipCummings.com

149

that over 70% of recipients will read that first before they read the body text.

4. **Keep it simple and straight.** Keep the message short and well formatted. Use correct spelling, double-check phone numbers or response web addresses, and send yourself a "test" e-mail to check the messages before sending to clients.

5. **Minimum 7 message rule.** Use a minimum of 7 messages in the series. Statistics show that it takes an average of 6 to 7 contacts before a customer acts. Use more messages in the series when possible, and space them at LEAST 2 to 3 days apart.

6. **Content, Content, Content.** Don't send a message just for the sake of sending a message. Make sure that there is content in the message. Include a free report, brochure, informational web link, or timely and interesting facts.

7. **Track The Databases.** Separate your databases (autoresponder lists) into at least 3 groups: past, present, and future customers. This allows you to track the success of the message series individually, as well as periodically send timely "broadcast" messages with different contexts to each list separately.

For a FREE 7-day course on "7 Steps To Building A Successful Marketing Plan," send an e-mail to ChipTips@ChipCummings.com

150

CHIP TIPS:

Here are your "personal road signs" from this Chapter:

1. We know it takes at least five contacts for the customer to remember you. Use autoresponders to create an automatic system that helps you regularly contact your prospects and customers with a minimum of work on your part. Autoresponder systems you can use include www.SimpleAutoresponders.com, Autoresponders.com, Autobots.net, and Automailer.com.

   Consult Autoresponder-Review.com for reviews and other valuable information about autoresponders.

2. The subject line is the headline for your message. Make sure you get it right because the recipient will not even open the message unless the subject catches their attention! Keep the headline short, intriguing, and use a verb whenever possible. Use words like "Discover," "Create," "Learn," "Develop," "Act," "Find Out" or put your subject line in the form of a question. Also, try to personalize the message by putting their first name in the subject line.

3. When you write the body text of your message, make sure you keep each line to no more than 65 characters by inserting a hard return (pressing "Enter") at the appropriate point in each line. This makes sure that the automatic word wrap feature on the recipient's computer won't garble your message.

For a FREE 7-day course on "7 Steps To Building A Successful Marketing Plan," send an e-mail to ChipTips@ChipCummings.com

151

4. Balance how many and how often you will send messages as part of your autoresponder sequence. Remember, you want to send enough messages to keep them engaged, but not so many that you irritate them. You want to time the messages far enough apart so as not to overwhelm them, but not so far apart that they forget why they requested the information from you in the first place. Strategies for creating an autoresponder series include packaging your autoresponder as a multi-part series of reports or as a series of online lessons for a course.

5. Organize your online database of e-mail addresses into three groups: future customers, present customers, and past customers. This helps you track the success of your autoresponders and allows you to customize your messages to each group.

For a FREE 7-day course on "7 Steps To Building A Successful Marketing Plan," send an e-mail to ChipTips@ChipCummings.com

152

Chapter 9

Reach Out and Touch Everyone

"Some of the world's greatest feats were accomplished by people not smart enough to know they were impossible."

Doug Larson

O ver the years, I have learned that developing a good referral system puts you on the road to steady, long-term success. To create effective at creating referrals, your post-marketing system must include a personal "contact" with each customer a minimum of four times per year. The very same concept applies to converting non-ready prospects into customers. I call this relationship marketing, and one of the best tools to accomplish this is through a newsletter.

Of course, traditional newsletters include a lot of problems and expenses — postage, printing, list management, delivery, returns, creation and content to name a few. Another more affordable and efficient option is using an electronic newsletter or what's called an e-zine. In this Chapter, we'll look at the process of setting up an electronic newsletter, as well as the use of a few other types of technology designed for mass communication with your customers including methods like teleconferences and Internet radio.

For a FREE 7-day course on "7 Steps To Building A Successful Marketing Plan," send an e-mail to ChipTips@ChipCummings.com

153

Publishing E-Zines

E-zines offer one of the easiest, most creative ways to get in front of a lot of customers on a regular basis. The "e-zine", which is short for electronic magazine, is a specially prepared, worded, and timed e-mail newsletter that you send to your prospects and customer base.

While regular newsletters (snail mail) can be effective for some, they can also be expensive, slow, and time consuming to prepare and mail. On the other hand, you can prepare electronic newsletters quickly, and inexpensively. I can send 50,000 e-mails at the touch of a button at virtually no cost! In many respects, customers are also more prone to read quick e-mails as opposed to lengthy paper newsletters, and you can measure the response and effectiveness of the newsletter (or offers and links contained within) immediately.

In some cases, you may want to develop different e-zines for different customer niches. I have several electronic newsletters that I distribute free-of-charge to over 90,000 people per month. Two of the most popular are "The Mortgage Minute" (www.TheMortgageMinute.com) which is provided to professionals within the mortgage lending industry, and "The e-Marketing Minute" (www.TheMarketingMinute.com) which is designed for sales professionals and distributed around the world. They are both free-of-charge, and anyone has the ability to subscribe through the above links or through my main website at www.ChipCummings.com.

Once set up, the entire e-zine process should take you about three hours per month to maintain and distribute. The first couple of times it will take you longer, but the returns are more than worth it. By communicating on a regular basis with your customers, you will protect your client base, build credibility, and create a following of new customers — all at a cost of practically zero!

For a FREE 7-day course on "7 Steps To Building A Successful Marketing Plan," send an e-mail to ChipTips@ChipCummings.com

154

Preparing your database

The first step is to prepare a database system which can at least track the subscribers name and e-mail address. You can capture e-zine subscriptions in both the online and offline worlds, but the easiest way is to capture online subscriptions by displaying a subscription form on your website which feeds directly into an autoresponder system. For your offline subscriptions, create an Excel spreadsheet that contains six columns: first name, last name, e-mail address, type of transaction, date of transaction, and update date.

Start by entering your current and past customers into the list. If you don't know your customer's e-mail address, start calling them and ask for it! Let them know that you appreciate their business, and as a valued customer you want to keep them up-to-date with a subscription to your e-zine. You can then enter this data directly into a web page subscription form, or enter it into an Excel spreadsheet and upload the names to your list hosting service. If you upload the list, most list hosting services will ask your customers to confirm their "opt in" status through an automatically generated e-mail message, so don't wait too long.

To comply with the "Do Not Call" regulations (see Chapter 12), if you have customers that you have not communicated with in over 18 months, you must send them a letter with some type of offer asking them to go to a website to enter their information, or asking them to call you directly. Such offers can include a drawing for a gift certificate, dinner, concert tickets, or a special affiliate report or conference call with one of your expert partners. Get creative, but make the value substantial enough to get your past customers to respond. It will be worth it if it means getting them back in the game.

For a FREE 7-day course on "7 Steps To Building A Successful Marketing Plan," send an e-mail to ChipTips@ChipCummings.com

155

Developing the content

Once you have a system in place to maintain the subscribers, the next step is to develop the actual newsletter. There are two formats you can use for creating your e-zine: basic text or HTML. In some cases, you may also want to incorporate audio and/or video components as part of the newsletter for added effect (see Chapter 10). I have come across a wide variety of formats, but there are advantages and disadvantages to them all. The advantage of regular text is that it displays on even the most basic computer system. Some customers use simple (or free) e-mail services that either can't display HTML in an e-mail message or they have turned the HTML feature off for various reasons. The advantage of HTML e-zines is they can use all the colors, graphics, and formatting available for web sites. However, in addition to the display issues mentioned above, some SPAM filters flag any HTML in a message as potential SPAM. To get around this, most systems allow you can create the same message or e-zine in both formats.

Other options are to create the e-zine as a PDF attachment, or create it as a separate newsletter webpage and link to it from an e-mail message. I use this last format for many of my e-zines to escape some of the constraints of the SPAM filters, and insure more consistent delivery.

Once you have selected the format, it's time to create the content. To create your e-zine, you can simply use Microsoft Word or another word processor. Select three or four topical issues of interest to your target market, taken from industry news sources, local resources, or personal experiences. Prepare a short piece on each topic which could include market information, personal and company highlights, a great customer story, or any number of other interesting elements.

Here's a tip: PERSONALIZE IT! Your personality should come through for the reader, so have some fun with it. But, keep

For a FREE 7-day course on "7 Steps To Building A Successful Marketing Plan," send an e-mail to ChipTips@ChipCummings.com

156

it short!   Customers ignore lengthy or hard to read e-mail messages, so make sure they can read your message within 2 to 3 minutes. Above all, make sure it contains good quality content.

You can also "hire" out the job of creating, writing and distributing the e-zine itself. There are several companies that provide this service, or you can search for a writer through an online "bid" service such as www.Elance.com.

For capturing the reader's attention, the most important part of the e-zine is the "header", or what appears in the subject line. Don't make it a sales pitch or cute. Instead, try to make it "catchy," short and to-the-point. If you need help creating your e-zine, there are several software packages which provide easy-to-use templates and graphics. To find these programs, you can search Google or one of the other search engines under "newsletter templates." One which I use and recommend is available at www.SimpleEzines.com.

Distributing your e-zine

You can distribute the actual e-zine through basic e-mail programs such as Outlook or ACT!, but I STRONGLY urge you to use a more detailed and comprehensive online list hosting service such as the SimpleAutoresponder.com site, Constant Contact, or Microsoft's bcentral.com. When you consider the time and effort required to track subscriptions and the possible liability factor, you realize this is not a do-it-yourself project. You can also use many other autoresponder systems to maintain your database of subscribers and to broadcast your e-zine.

Whatever system you use, you must provide subscribers the ability to "opt-out" of the service at anytime. Others should be able to sign up (i.e. opt-in) electronically, either from a link in the e-zine itself, through an e-mail submission, or the preferred method — through your website or a dedicated webpage. Many of the online

For a FREE 7-day course on "7 Steps To Building A Successful Marketing Plan," send an e-mail to ChipTips@ChipCummings.com

157

list maintenance companies provide free hosting and upload/ download capabilities from your Excel spreadsheet. You can find other services with more options for less than $15 per month.

In addition, you should encourage customers to forward the e-zine on to their friends and associates, and they will! As the list of subscribers grows, so will your exposure and credibility which leads to more referrals.

To increase your distribution, you can also list your e-zine in online e-zine directories. One of the largest and best known directories is the Directory of E-zines, run by Charlie Page. You can find them at www.DirectoryofEzines.com.

Another way you can increase your distribution is to place "classified" advertisements in other people's e-zines and newsletters. Look for complimentary publications and issues of interest to your target market, and offer to "swap" links or to place a small 2 to 3 line ad. The cost is usually minimal ($5-$50) depending on the size of the e-zine's subscriber base.

Adding links & offers

As you become more comfortable formatting your newsletter, add links back to your website and links to other interesting sites, articles or information. You can even market affiliate services and products with special discounts or offers.

If you decide to use a list hosting company, you can measure your e-mail traffic to determine effectiveness as well as the popularity of each link or offer within the e-zine. This allows you to track your customers' preferences and improve your newsletter. The e-zine should also allow readers to respond directly back to you (via e-mail) with comments, questions, concerns, or any other customer service issue.

For a FREE 7-day course on "7 Steps To Building A Successful Marketing Plan," send an e-mail to ChipTips@ChipCummings.com

158

SPAM Issues

Everyone hates SPAM, so there are a couple of rules that will keep you in good graces with your subscribers and with your list hosting company. First, NEVER purchase any e-mail lists unless it's a qualified opt-in affiliated business partner list. Otherwise, the quality of these lists will always be poor, and the liability risks are very high. Respond to any subscriber complaints quickly and always have your contact information on every e-zine.

However you decide to collect names for your subscriber list, keep in mind that you have to be able to prove that each person opted-in to your e-zine mailing database. Also, as mentioned earlier, you must also provide a no-hassle way for subscribers to opt-out. This is a key reason why you should use a list hosting service, since they manage these functions automatically.

There are a few other ways you can avoid getting accused of spamming. Many online list hosting services let you upload names into your online database, which then automatically sends an e-mail asking each person on the list to confirm their subscription. This provides an audit trail in case you are accused of spamming someone in your list. You can also implement a "double opt-in" system which requires that people who sign up confirm their decision to subscribe. With a double opt-in system you will lose some subscribers, but the quality of the list will be much higher. You should also make sure you alert customers to add an exclusion to their e-mail SPAM filtering software based on your e-mail address. Then, to make sure your e-zine is regularly delivered, keep the "from" e-mail address in your messages consistent.

For a FREE 7-day course on "7 Steps To Building A Successful Marketing Plan," send an e-mail to ChipTips@ChipCummings.com

159

Delivering Teleconferences

Another way you can reach out and touch your customers is with teleconferences. In a teleconference, participants call into a conference center at a specified time and you host an interview or make your presentation over the phone from the convenience of your home or office. Some conference service companies offer voice only facilities over the phone network or a combination of telephone and synchronized PowerPoint presentations through a web site. Still others, such as the Webex system (www.webex.com), offer simultaneous video links as well.

When you do a voice-only teleconference, the presentation is similar to a radio broadcast. Most service providers offer features like the ability to include two-way communications in a question and answer format, the ability to mute the participants (quite handy if someone's dog is barking in the background), recording features, and several other options. Even with voice-only presentations, you can distribute handouts prior to the presentation via e-mail or your website.

Unless you have the equipment and the telephone lines to conduct this kind of seminar yourself, you should definitely use a conference service provider. For regular users, these service providers usually charge a flat monthly fee, or you can opt to pay a per-line charge for single events. Since there is cost involved, you have to decide if you want to charge for the seminar or offer it free as a form of advertising for your business. Some of the providers of these services include Voicetext.com, Black and White Communications, KRM Services (krm.com), Accuconference (accuconference.com), and Webex.com. I provide regular teleconferences regarding marketing strategies, and to find out more, visit www.TheMarketingMinute.com.

For a FREE 7-day course on "7 Steps To Building A Successful Marketing Plan," send an e-mail to ChipTips@ChipCummings.com

160

Internet Radio Shows

Imagine hosting your own radio show, without the need for a license, and without geographical boundaries! There are hundreds of new radio stations being added every year and they're all looking for content. Unlike regular radio, the Internet provides the potential for highly targeted radio programs. Internet radio stations seek two things when they start a new show: First, they seek someone who is connected to an online community. If you have an e-newsletter, host a listserv, or manage a message board for a particular community, you can make the case that you are a good candidate for an Internet talk radio show. Second, they look for a community that has a recognizable market for products sold to that community. This allows them to pay for the show with targeted advertising.

One place you can start with this idea is www.wsradio.com. This group produces internet talk radio programs including many business programs. You can propose your own show idea by contacting Lee Mirabal, V.P. of Programming at leemirabal@wsradio.com or 858-623-0199 ext 101.

I also have my OWN Internet radio station (or what's known as "podcasting"), which you can listen in on at www.PersonalPowerRadio.com!

This allows me to have 24/7 worldwide broadcasting for only a couple hundred bucks per month.

For a FREE 7-day course on "7 Steps To Building A Successful Marketing Plan," send an e-mail to ChipTips@ChipCummings.com

161

CHIP TIPS:

Here are your "personal road signs" from this Chapter:

1. E-zines offer one of the easiest, most creative ways to get in front of many customers on a regular basis, providing a platform for continued relationship marketing. There are two ways to capture e-zine subscriptions: online and offline. You can capture e-zine subscriptions online by displaying a subscription form on your website. Offline, create an Excel spreadsheet that contains six columns: first name, last name, e-mail address, type of transaction, date of transaction, and update date. Then, upload this list to your list hosting service.

2. There are two formats you can use to develop the content for your e-zine: basic text or HTML. Basic text has fewer bells and whistles, but guarantees that your e-zine will display on any recipient computer system. HTML allows you to make your e-zine more visually appealing, but some recipients may not be able to display your e-zine. To address both audiences, you can distribute the same e-zine in both formats (basic text and HTML). Software packages, like the one provided at www.SimpleEzines.com can help you create your e-zine.

3. Keep your e-zine short! Customers ignore messages that are too lengthy, so make sure they can read it within 2 to 3 minutes. Add links back to your website and links to other interesting sites, articles or information. You can even market affiliate services and products with special discounts or offers. The most important part of the e-zine is what appears in the subject line. Make the subject line short and to-the-point.

For a FREE 7-day course on "7 Steps To Building A Successful Marketing Plan," send an e-mail to ChipTips@ChipCummings.com

162

4. The most efficient and safe way to distribute your e-zine is by using a list hosting service such as Microsoft's bcentral.com. You might also be able to use the broadcast feature of your autoresponder system.

5. Whatever distribution system you use, you must provide subscribers the ability to "opt-out" of the service at anytime. This makes it easy for the recipient to get off your list and covers you for any SPAM legal issues. You can also avoid SPAM Legal issues by asking subscribers to electronically confirm their subscription. This provides an additional audit trail in case you are accused of spamming someone in your online or offline list. You should also alert customers to add exclusions to their SPAM filtering based on your sending e-mail address. For this reason, make sure you keep the same "from" e-mail address.

6. Two additional ways to reach out to your target audience is through teleconferences & Internet radio. In a teleconference, participants call into a conference center at a specified time and you make your presentation over the phone. Some conference service companies offer voice only facilities over the phone network, or a combination of telephone and synchronized PowerPoint presentations through a web site. Some providers in this area include KRM Services (krm.com), Accuconference (accuconference.com), and webex.com.

Internet radio offers you the chance to host a radio show broadcast through the Internet. Internet radio producers are looking for people who are connected to an online community that has a recognizable market for products sold to that community. One place you can start is wsradio.com.

For a FREE 7-day course on "7 Steps To Building A Successful Marketing Plan," send an e-mail to ChipTips@ChipCummings.com

163

For a FREE 7-day course on "7 Steps To Building A Successful Marketing Plan," send an e-mail to ChipTips@ChipCummings.com

164

Chapter 10

Can You Hear Me?

"If you are wedded to today's trends, you'll be widowed by the weekend."

E. Stanley Jones

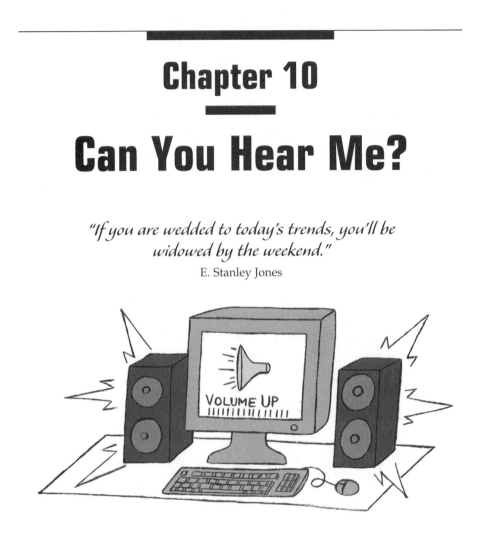

I magine picking up the phone, dialing a phone number, and leaving a short voice mail message. No big deal, right? What if you could take that voice mail message and put it on your web site within 90 seconds? Or attach it to an e-mail with a simple "cut and paste?" All this without having to know anything about programming, without hosting the audio files on your web site, or installing "special plug-ins" for anyone who wanted to hear your message. That would be a powerful marketing tool!

For a FREE 7-day course on "7 Steps To Building A Successful Marketing Plan," send an e-mail to ChipTips@ChipCummings.com

165

A new technology which simplifies the process was recently revolutionized by a former Microsoft developer. With this technology, you can use audio as an effective (yet simple) marketing tool. It provides another way to build long-term success and separate yourself further from the competition — all while developing a strong personal customer relationship.

So What Is It?

Creating audio files or video clips and placing them within a web site is certainly not new technology. However, up till now, it was a cumbersome and cost prohibitive exercise for most small businesses. First, you had to create the sound files with certain equipment and store them in a directory on your website or create a sizable e-mail attachment. Then, anyone who wanted to hear the audio had to have the right software loaded on their computer. If the listener didn't have the appropriate software, they would have to go through a download process, and then wait to hear the message. Then it might take 15 to 45 seconds to download the file before they even hear anything — an eternity on the Internet! With the typical Internet surfer having an attention span of approximately 5 to 7 seconds, this type of delay could result in a lost sale or missed opportunities. So, from a practical standpoint, the marketing applications for audio and video were quite limited unless you were in the category of a Disney or General Motors.

Things are different now. Rick Raddatz, a creator of the Instant Audio system, has simplified the whole audio transmission process making it as simple to use as dialing the phone. What makes this technology so new is the fact that you and the person listening to your audio don't need any special software or any special downloads and you don't need any space on your web site. Your customers and prospects can play back the audio instantly within seconds! I personally use this technology for many different

For a FREE 7-day course on "7 Steps To Building A Successful Marketing Plan," send an e-mail to ChipTips@ChipCummings.com

166

applications within dozens of websites, and have found it to be inexpensive and as easily to use as dialing the telephone! I simply dial an 800 number (or a similar number for international callers), record a message, and then paste a link in my web site or e-mail. You can also upload other types of recordings, such as interviews, radio or television clips, songs or long dissertations! Of course, you need to make sure you avoid copy-written work.

It's simple to use — the first audio message I recorded took me about 90 seconds to implement! To experience it yourself, go to any of my websites such as www.ChipCummings.com or the site for this book at www.StopSellingandStartListening.com! For a free detailed report and to try this service for free, go to www.Instant-Talking-Website.com.

Audio Strategies

So, how can we use this new tool in our overall marketing strategy? The varieties of marketing possibilities are staggering. Here are just a few ways you can start using this technology right away:

Web site Welcome Message

Your website is your business home on the Internet. When people visit, you can welcome them inside and greet them with a warm personal message that thanks them for visiting, and directs their attention to any special areas of interest on the web page. A short personal greeting also gives you the opportunity to let them hear, directly from your mouth, things like your UVP (Unique Value Proposition), general items about your company, and the products and services you offer. Your voice has far more impact than just printed words on a page. You can either configure the message to play immediately when they enter the web site (or a particular web page), or you

For a FREE 7-day course on "7 Steps To Building A Successful Marketing Plan," send an e-mail to ChipTips@ChipCummings.com

167

can provide a button that allows the visitor to control when they want to play the message.

As an example, here's a sample message that could play automatically when a visitor opens a web site for a real estate office:

> *"Hi! This is Karen Walters, owner and President of Walters Real Estate, and I would like to welcome you to our "Showcase Of Homes."*
>
> *We have had the privilege of serving the greater Tampa area for over 32 years now, and have one of the most experienced real estate teams in the entire state.*
>
> *Please look around at the many fine homes we have to offer, and you can click on each one for a guided tour. If you don't see the home of your dreams here, don't panic! Our dedicated team of professionals has access to the largest database of homes from throughout the state.*
>
> *Thanks again for visiting, and we look forward to helping you move into the home of your dreams......"*

While anyone could certainly read this on a web page, the impact is far greater if they were to hear it directly from Karen while they start to look over the web site.

Product & Service Information

Wouldn't it be nice to have the ability to personally describe different aspects of your products and services? Here are just a few suggestions from a variety of industries:

Real Estate

Listing Descriptions: Yes, pictures tell a thousand words, but the impact is 100 times greater when they also hear you describe

For a FREE 7-day course on "7 Steps To Building A Successful Marketing Plan," send an e-mail to ChipTips@ChipCummings.com

168

the real estate listing. Your audio can provide insights into why the owner is selling; what's in the neighborhood; what school district or area the property is located in; how far from the highway, etc.

Home Features: You can verbally walk them through the house and describe the rooms and beautiful woodwork. Describe features when the pictures just don't do it justice. Is there a home warranty? Or how about carpeting or decorating allowance. Video applications (described later in this Chapter) can sell a house through a virtual tour from thousands of miles away.

Open House Schedules: Tell a customer when they can view the home and exactly how to find it so they won't get lost! What about other times they can see it? Is it on a "Parade of Homes" tour? Video clips could show them the neighborhood, schools, or landmarks.

Price Enhancements: Has the listing price recently been lowered? What about other included items such as a home warranty or 2nd refrigerator located in the garage? Describe how it relates to other similarly priced homes in the neighborhood.

Office Locations: How many offices do you have and where are they located? Can they visit during weekends or evenings? Do you have other services on-site such as mortgage lending, title companies, or home improvement/repair firms? You can provide answers to these questions in a personal and inviting fashion, beyond what mere written words can express.

Mortgage Lending

Interest Rates: Allow customers to not only see the current interest rates, but to hear your analysis of why they are going up or down and any special pricing incentives you may be offering. What is the Federal Reserve doing and why? How does the bond market control the pattern of rates?

For a FREE 7-day course on "7 Steps To Building A Successful Marketing Plan," send an e-mail to ChipTips@ChipCummings.com

169

Loan Programs: Take the opportunity to personally explain how 3/1 ARM program relates to a 5/1 ARM or a fixed rate program. Talk about how they can qualify and what information is needed for a loan. Walk them through the costs, credit requirements, and explain Truth In Lending and other documents in a personal way just as you would during a face-to-face application! Video clips can actually walk them through the application process online, showing them what to fill out and where.

Promotional Incentives: Describe your home improvement programs or bridge loans. Do you offer a construction lending program? Is there a benefit for having you handle both loans? Do you have any special pricing for self-employed borrowers? Are you giving away free appraisals? These are items you can communicate through vocal excitement like no printed words can!

First-time Homebuyer Options: First-time homebuyers need special personal attention. Use your audios to explain complicated terms and walk them through the process to let them feel comfortable with the transaction. Explain special programs and available low, no down-payment options.

Insurance Services

Policy Descriptions: Explain the difference in coverage options and what happens when an insurance plan and participants are evaluated. Do they need a good credit rating? People visiting an insurance web site feel more comfortable when they hear the answers as opposed to reading them.

Rider/Term Options: Let them know if they can get a discount for multiple types of coverage and what sorts of terms are available. Are there waiting periods before they can be accepted? Describe the coverage limits and how you will come to their aid filing claims and forms in times of need.

For a FREE 7-day course on "7 Steps To Building A Successful Marketing Plan," send an e-mail to ChipTips@ChipCummings.com

170

Rating Information: Take a moment to inform customers about the stability of the company backing the policy. What exclusions are there and do different companies cover certain damages better?

Retail Stores

Product Descriptions: Describe the products you stock and whether you are the exclusive dealer. What different colors or sizes are available and does it require a special order? Use audio to personalize their use of the product as they view it on the web site, or video clips to provide a demonstration!

Use Information: What other uses are there for this product? Do you have any customer recommendations or restricted uses? By playing personal audio messages associated with a product, you can provide a "3-dimensional" view into how they can benefit from their purchase.

Availability: Do you ship the merchandise the same day? Can they expect it within a week? What about return policies and refunds? Printed information doesn't always provide the confidence that a friendly voice does.

Restaurants

Featured Menus: Describe the atmosphere and add emotion and accent to the site. People might be more inclined to visit a German restaurant that is presented with a German accent and flair. Spotlight the chef, the quite peaceful décor, or the restaurant's convenience to local attractions. You can describe reservation policies and landmarks to help them find you.

Reviews and Awards: What's the latest from the food critics? You can emphasize the "Best In Seafood" award that you won

For a FREE 7-day course on "7 Steps To Building A Successful Marketing Plan," send an e-mail to ChipTips@ChipCummings.com

171

last month. Have the chef personally describe a dish and create a mouth-watering experience right online! Videos can create mouth-watering images that generate new traffic.

Daily Specials: Are there special menus or dishes during the week? How about the Sunday brunch or sports bar specials before the big game? Do you have carry-out or delivery services? Personal voice descriptions add a lot when you're trying to lure hungry customers.

Attorney or Accounting Services

Special Areas of Practice: Do you service specific niche markets such as product liability or workers compensation law? Do you have the capacity to handle Department of Housing and Urban Development Audits or specialize in tax appeals? Audio allows you to explain your experience, communicate confidence and elicit action from your prospects.

Explanation of Terms: Are there confusing terms or language that you can clarify for your customers? Talk about a recent change in the tax code or state probate requirements in a simple, straight-forward way that makes clients feel comfortable about asking those "stupid questions" in a non-threatening environment.

Customer Announcements: Who are your prominent clients and what have you done for them that could relate to the prospect?

Multi-level or Network marketing Opportunities

Selling The Opportunity: Do you need an effective way to communicate with down-lines, or describe new products and services? What are some of the latest numbers or recruiting

For a FREE 7-day course on "7 Steps To Building A Successful Marketing Plan," send an e-mail to ChipTips@ChipCummings.com

172

strategies? Audio and video clips help you share success stories, member news and information, and customer appreciation events in a fun and informative fashion!

Audio Postcards

Another aspect of creating audio messages is to combine them with a quick printed message such as an "Audio Postcard." This technology allows you to create and send these personal postcard messages as easily as generating e-mail! This technique is not only new and revolutionary, but saves on postage!

Here is a quick example of an audio postcard:

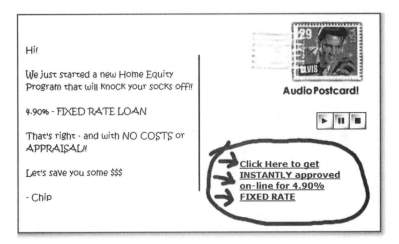

Anyone who made it onto on any of my database lists or who has subscribed to one of my many e-zines has undoubtedly seen a few creative postcards from me! Now I'm getting ready to implement video postcards as well!

The advantage of the audio postcard is that it provides the customer with a brief message in writing *and* reinforces the message with audio, plus combines a link that can go to any web page you wish! Direct the prospect or customer right into an application, a sales event, promotion, or special report.

For a FREE 7-day course on "7 Steps To Building A Successful Marketing Plan," send an e-mail to ChipTips@ChipCummings.com

173

Customer Testimonials

There is nothing more powerful than a testimonial from a happy customer (or several!). Let them say it themselves on your web site, next to their written words, for a truly powerful impact. Written testimonials just cannot relay the joy, excitement and satisfaction of satisfied customers like an audio message. The audio system (www.InstantTalkingWebsite.com) provides an easy way for customers to call a toll-free number and record their testimonial at their convenience. Then you can simple cut and paste it into your website, or forward it to your computer specialist. Messages only need to be posted once, and you can change the recording as often as you wish without having to change the website page or e-mail.

E-Mail Signature Files

A personalized e-mail signature is still one of the most under-utilized marketing opportunities. An e-mail signature is something you add to the end of your e-mail message which acts like your electronic business card. In addition to simple text, you can attach a quick personal audio message as a tag line to every one of your e-mail messages, or link it to an Audio Postcard or video file for added impact.

E-zines

As we discussed in Chapter 9, I use several e-zines to reach customers, prospects, affinity marketing groups, and others. You can include personal audio comments, testimonials, product information, service announcements, event information, or staff introductions right in the e-zine itself. For an added twist, incorporate video clips embedded in an e-zine!

For a FREE 7-day course on "7 Steps To Building A Successful Marketing Plan," send an e-mail to ChipTips@ChipCummings.com

174

Autoresponder Series

Imagine being able to send a personal voice message to your customers and prospects as part of an auto responder series. I have used this many times, and in some cases, the response rates jump by more than 200%! In Chapter 8, I talked about the power of using autoresponders to turn suspects into prospects, and how to use attachments with free reports as a value-added service. Now it's possible to personalize the reports with messages and instructional audio to make a greater impact.

Relationship (Affinity) Marketing Strategies

Create personal messages for cross-marketing opportunities with your affinity partners, such as real estate agents, mortgage loan officers, attorneys, financial planners, accountants, etc. Record and exchange personal introductions and place them on each other's web sites, or introduce new products and services from partners that compliment yours!

Photo Descriptions

Take any photo or graphic image and place a recorded message along side that someone can play to learn about a new product, changes to existing products, or educational programs for customers.

Personal Bio & Qualifications

Think of creating a resume on-line and then adding you own voice to emphasize your qualifications! Personal conviction and emotion come through clearly when the client or prospect can hear the difference between you and the competition.

For a FREE 7-day course on "7 Steps To Building A Successful Marketing Plan," send an e-mail to ChipTips@ChipCummings.com

175

Team & Customer Service Introductions

Use audio messaging to introduce your support team, or key staff. Let your team member's record personal messages to help strengthen your personal commitment to customer service and add credibility to your operation. It's nice when customers can put a "face with a name" when they talk to someone on the phone!

Education and Entertainment Events

Explain details of educational programs, instructional materials or forms, or various learning expectations. Create enthusiasm for company picnics, sporting events, or rallies.

Guarantees and Warranty Information

What personal service guarantees do you provide? Way beyond the written word, people can hear sincerity in your voice. Will you be there if the customer experiences problems or has any service concerns? What are the specifics on returned items, broken items, or lousy customer service? People will tend to believe you more when they hear you say it.

Special Sales or Discounts

Are you running a special on end-of-season or discontinued merchandise? Do preferred customers get a discount? Combine this with a quick audio postcard or a video clip to get instant results.

Locations and Directions

Where are your offices located? Are they near the mall or particularly hard to find? Can you give me directions such as "down three lights, and past the McDonalds, you'll see our sign on the right side..."

For a FREE 7-day course on "7 Steps To Building A Successful Marketing Plan," send an e-mail to ChipTips@ChipCummings.com

176

Privacy Statements

Personal privacy and the safeguarding of customer information has become an increasing concern. Record a personal privacy statement and attach it to your site or welcome page to make customers feel confident that you respect their confidential information. Make sure you cover any licensing restrictions or geographical limitations as well.

Implementing audio for your business

Now that you know some of the basic ways to create and build customer confidence using audio, lets talk about how you can implement this technology. You can find the system I use is at www.Instant-Talking-Website.com. Here you can try it for free (I'll refund your dollar!), and attend free teleconferences I host, where I teach you how to implement the strategies!

Once you have signed up for the service, you can call the toll-free number, enter your account number (which they will assign and send you instantly via e-mail), and record your first message. Before recording your message, I recommend that you write out a script of the entire message. Make it conversational and practice it a few times so that it sounds natural. Make sure to smile and "laugh with your voice" to create an upbeat feeling for the listener. After you record your message, you log onto the main web site where you can select the message you just recorded, then select how you want to publish your audio. Your choices include audio for your web site, audio postcards, audio for an eBay sale, creating templates, or using audio for an e-mail message.

Once you select how you want to publish your audio, the web site lets you configure how you want the audio presented. You can select control button formats and colors. You can also select

For a FREE 7-day course on "7 Steps To Building A Successful Marketing Plan," send an e-mail to ChipTips@ChipCummings.com

177

whether you want the audio to automatically play or wait for the visitor to click the on-screen control. There are hundreds of combinations, and you are limited only by your imagination! Once you set up the audio and what it should look like (and how you decide to use it), the system generates HTML code that you can cut and paste into your web site or e-mail.

Try it out, and you'll be amazed how easy it is to generate a whole variety of messages!

Implementing video for your business

Just as implementing audio has gotten much simpler, video has done the same. It is now possible to record a clip on a basic camcorder, and within minutes have it available on your website or as an e-mail attachment! Although I am just starting to experiment with this process, the implications are tremendous!

Not only can you provide actual product or service demonstrations, but the process will redefine online education and interactive marketing. The key lies in a special file format which compresses the size of the file and makes the viewing instant and seamless — even for viewers that have slow dial-up modem connections!

With a digital camcorder (that has downloadable capabilities through a "fire wire" or similar connection), you can easily store the file on a computer or on a website. To make it viewable for a visitor, you need to use a file converter and compression utility that will convert it into FLASH format (FLV). The best utility I have found for this process is available from Sorenson Media (www.sorenson.com) called Sorenson Squeeze. To view examples of how this can revolutionize a website, take a look at the examples provided at http://www.macromedia.com/cfusion/showcase/index.cfm.

For a FREE 7-day course on "7 Steps To Building A Successful Marketing Plan," send an e-mail to ChipTips@ChipCummings.com

178

For those who are looking for a simpler solution, you can record a clip directly from aPC equipped with a "web cam" and a microphone, and without any software or experience, cut and paste a single line of code to have a video message added to a website or e-mail message. You can find more information about this technique at www.SimpleVideoWebsites.com.

For a FREE 7-day course on "7 Steps To Building A Successful Marketing Plan," send an e-mail to ChipTips@ChipCummings.com

179

CHIP TIPS:

Here are your "personal road signs" from this Chapter:

1. Using audio as a marketing tool provides another way to build long-term success and separate yourself from the competition while developing a personal customer relationship.

2. With Internet audio technology, you and the person listening to your audio don't need any special software and you don't need any space on your web site. You simply dial an 800 number, record a message, and then paste a link in your web site or e-mail. Your customers and prospects can play back the audio instantaneously from your web site or e-mail message.

3. Uses for online audio include web site welcome messages, product and service information, audio postcards, customer testimonials, e-mail signature files, audio e-zines, links from auto-responders, cross-marketing with affiliates, photo descriptions, resume and qualifications, team introductions, education and entertainment, guarantee and warranty information, description of special sales or discounts, verbal directions to your office, and disclosure of privacy statements.

4. One of the best systems for Internet audio is AudioGenerator (AudioGenerator.com). After you record your message via a toll-free phone number, you log on to

For a FREE 7-day course on "7 Steps To Building A Successful Marketing Plan," send an e-mail to ChipTips@ChipCummings.com

180

their web site and configure the message depending on how you want to distribute it (web site, audio postcard, audio for an eBay sale, or audio for an e-mail message). Then their system provides you with HTML code that you can paste into your web site or e-mail. This code provides the link that the listener clicks on to hear your message.

For a FREE 7-day course on "7 Steps To Building A Successful Marketing Plan," send an e-mail to ChipTips@ChipCummings.com

181

For a FREE 7-day course on "7 Steps To Building A Successful Marketing Plan," send an e-mail to ChipTips@ChipCummings.com

182

Chapter 11

e-Strategies — Tradition With a Twist

"Since there is nothing new under the sun, creativity means simply putting old things together in a fresh way."

Sherwood E. Wirt

You're driving down the road. All of the sudden, you hit a traffic jam and come to a dead stop. There's a roadblock up ahead, and nobody seems to know exactly which way to go. There are a few signs indicating a "detour," but everybody is trying to get down the same one-lane road and progress is slow.

Remember the last time you found yourself in that situation? It's frustrating to say the least, but your first inclination is to search for other ways to get around the traffic tie-up. Unfortunately, most salespeople don't respond the same way when it comes to their future.

Everybody hits roadblocks now and then. The difference with a Top Producer is that they are always prepared with five alternate routes to get around them! They don't sit there and complain or get out to "commiserate" with other average salespeople. Nor do they sit there and wait for the situation to change. Instead, they take charge and change the situation!

For a FREE 7-day course on "7 Steps To Building A Successful Marketing Plan," send an e-mail to ChipTips@ChipCummings.com

183

Top Producers always have multiple marketing strategies in play at any time, and integrate them with one another. In this chapter, we'll explore multiple ways to generate traffic, drive prospects to your websites, and how to capture e-mail contact information. Part of the secret is to put a technological twist on some of the more "traditional" forms of marketing you're doing now!

Creating an Integrated Marketing Message

The problem with the way most businesses use traditional advertising is that they do not integrate it with their other marketing strategies. Advertising is useless if it doesn't present your UVP (Unique Value Proposition) and stimulate the

For a FREE 7-day course on "7 Steps To Building A Successful Marketing Plan," send an e-mail to ChipTips@ChipCummings.com

184

prospect to take some sort of action. For example, most ads in the Yellow Pages only state what the business does, instead of illustrating the value that it provides. To make matters worse, these ads usually don't even include a website address. So, the ad looks just like dozens of others on the same page and subsequently generates a low response.

On the other hand, integrated advertising makes sure all your marketing efforts work together to drive your prospects to the same place, and creates a uniform message and market identity. What if your Yellow Pages ad, direct mail, magazine ad, and business card targeted for a particular niche all announced that a free report (or some other value offer) written specifically for that audience was available at your websites? These are all very different means of marketing, but the message is integrated, and you present an immediate value to the prospect in return for their action (i.e. free report, sample, gift, etc.). As people respond to this offer, you continue to feed new prospects into your online database system after they sign up to receive your "Personal Value." This way, you not only collect their contact information in one place, but by using codes or special HTML links, you also track the success of your various marketing methods.

31 Traditional Strategies with a Twist!

So how many ways can you integrate your marketing message? It is limited only by your creativity and imagination, but to get you started, here are 31 ways to use some traditional methods with an added twist. The twist is integration. You will integrate all these techniques with Internet technology through your website, and with other marketing methods you use to obtain a Prospect's name and e-mail contact information.

You certainly don't have to implement all these methods. My goal is to provide a buffet of ideas and stimulate some creative

For a FREE 7-day course on "7 Steps To Building A Successful Marketing Plan," send an e-mail to ChipTips@ChipCummings.com

185

thinking on your part so you can choose those that work best for you. Start with five key ideas that you can put into play now. Whichever ones you pursue, make sure you have multiple response triggers available to prompt a reaction from Prospects!

1. Customer check-ups

Chip's rule is that you need to touch your past and present customers at least six times a year. One great way you can do this is to offer a customer check-up once or twice a year. Dentists and mechanics have done this for years. Many dentists send out postcards reminding people that it's time for their six month check-up. Some mechanics also send a notice to their customers that their car is due for an oil change. You can use this same strategy. For example, in my business, I contact my customers once a year to schedule what I call a "financial physical" where we examine where they are financially and make sure they are on the right track. They may not need any of my services immediately, but I am always going to be first on their list when the time comes — or when a friend or associate is in need!

Use your autoresponder system to automatically send an e-mail notice once or twice a year to let your customers know that it's time for their check-up. Either have the autoresponder copy you on the message or have your CRM (Customer Relationship Management) software remind you who's up for a check-up so you can follow-up with a phone call. Don't mistakenly believe that this strategy diverts your attention away from creating sales. On the contrary, it will enhance sales by reinforcing the relationship.

Listen to how often your customers are telling you they need to hear from you!

For a FREE 7-day course on "7 Steps To Building A Successful Marketing Plan," send an e-mail to ChipTips@ChipCummings.com

186

2. Professional roundtables

Another way you can touch your customers and add value is to offer free professional roundtables to your customers. When you host a professional roundtable, you partner up with an affiliated business or professional to host an event. Your customers have a chance to hear a presentation and ask questions of an expert on a subject of interest to them. For years, we provided "Lunch & Learn" events which became wildly popular!

For example, a real estate agent may partner up with a landscaper to do a presentation on tips for "landscaping your home for under $500." The great thing about planning an event like this is that you can leverage the contact lists of at least two parties: you and the expert speaker. In this example the expert is the landscaper. If you have the event at the facility of a third party, say a Home Depot or a local nursery, you can leverage the venue provider's publicity for the event as well. Why would other parties get involved in this? Because as a recognized expert, you're bringing them targeted prospects!

The best way to leverage technology to manage a professional roundtable is to offer to handle the registration for the event, via a special web page, with a form to capture an e-mail address. Present the event as a special benefit for your customers and make sure they understand that they must sign up to attend. Use an autoresponder to confirm their registration and send them directions and reminders as the date for the event draws close.

Provide the web page link information to the sign-up page for your event partners so they can contact their customers as well. If they contact their own customers, you don't risk compromising their customer privacy policies, and their credibility will generate a higher response rate. As long as you make it clear that you are co-hosting the event, it's acceptable for you to collect their contact information when they sign up. You

For a FREE 7-day course on "7 Steps To Building A Successful Marketing Plan," send an e-mail to ChipTips@ChipCummings.com

187

will have to negotiate with your presentation partners how much attendee contact information you will share. Will you only share information from those attendees who are their customers or will you share the entire list with all the parties? If you do share the entire list with all the parties, make sure this does not conflict with anyone's stated customer privacy policy.

At the event, provide each participant with a free gift. Preferably, this should be something clever that will help them remember you and the event. In addition to this, tell the attendees that if they provide their contact information, you will send them a free report related to the event. This provides an opportunity to collect accurate contact information at the event, and creates another excuse to contact the attendees.

3. Teleconferences

Teleconferences are similar to professional roundtables, but instead of making the presentation in person, you conduct the event over the phone. This is particularly effective if you and your presentation partners have a geographically diverse audience, or you are reaching an audience that is time pressed to attend an event in person. I hold dozens of teleconferences for a variety of target markets.

The biggest advantage of teleconferences is that they are convenient for you, your presentation partners, and the attendees. Anyone involved in the event can participate by simply dialing the telephone. Another advantage is that you can record the event and offer the recording after the event. This creates another opportunity to contact the participants.

The technology you employ to get the word out about your teleconference is very similar to that for the professional roundtable. You can use your autoresponder to provide the telephone number and access code when attendees sign up.

For a FREE 7-day course on "7 Steps To Building A Successful Marketing Plan," send an e-mail to ChipTips@ChipCummings.com

188

Some teleconference service providers include VoiceText (www.VoiceText.com), KRM Services (www.KRM.com), Accuconference (www.Accuconference.com), and Webex (www.Webex.com). Chapter 9 discussed delivering teleconferences in greater detail.

4. Fax broadcast

Although e-mail has stolen much of the thunder from fax machines, there is still a good use for this technology. Similar to an e-mail list, when you broadcast a fax, you have one document that you fax to a large group all at one time. This works best for highly graphic information that is time sensitive or forms that require a signature. Due to government regulations restricting unsolicited faxes, you can only use this marketing method with your existing customers that have specifically provided you with their fax number, or are inherently part of a group such as an association or membership club.

There are three basic ways you can broadcast a fax. First, if you have an advanced fax machine, it may let you store recipient phone numbers and fax to the stored list. This however, can be expensive and time consuming because the fax machine ties up your phone line as it methodically dials each number. The second method is to use a fax modem in your PC, but it has the same issues as a fax machine trying to broadcast a fax. The best method is to use an online fax service. With this method, you send your document electronically to the fax service along with downloading a list of fax phone numbers. Then the fax service delivers the fax to the list at a preset date and time. Some fax service vendors include eFax (eFax.com), Data on Call (DataOnCall.com), and Voice Text (VoiceText.com). For a more up-to-date list of vendors, check the resources section of my websites at www.ChipCummings.com.

For a FREE 7-day course on "7 Steps To Building A Successful Marketing Plan," send an e-mail to ChipTips@ChipCummings.com

189

5. Voice broadcast

Similar to a fax broadcast, a voice broadcast delivers a recorded message to your customers by dialing a list of phone numbers. This method actually works better if the recipient isn't there to pick up the phone, and having the broadcast record the message onto their answering system. If they do pick up the phone, an alternate recording informs them that they have a message from you waiting for them. This is much less annoying than picking up the phone expecting to talk to a person and getting a recording instead.

As with fax broadcast, and due to "Do Not Call" regulations, I recommend you only use it for your existing customers. It's particularly useful when you need to communicate changing information on short notice. For example, I've used this method to let customers know about important changes in mortgage rates, or details for upcoming events. Two vendors I've used for this type of service include Information Now (800service.com) and Arch Telecom. Check the resource section of my websites (ChipCummings.com) for an update on other service providers.

6. Voice recordings

If voice broadcast is a "push" method of advertising, using a voice recording on an 800 number is the "pull" version. With this method, rather than broadcasting a voice message to your customers, you let them know that you have a free report that they can retrieve by calling an 800 number.

This provides another convenient way for prospects to respond to your offer if they can't (or won't) immediately access the Internet. Interestingly enough, another advantage to this method is that if you're offering a free report, people would rather call an 800 number with a recording than risk encountering a live salesperson who might try to "sell" them something. When they call to hear

For a FREE 7-day course on "7 Steps To Building A Successful Marketing Plan," send an e-mail to ChipTips@ChipCummings.com

190

your message, you can instruct them to either leave their contact information as a voice message, or direct them to a website where they can enter their contact information to receive the report.

7. Cooperative marketing with competitors

No matter how good you are at what you do, you can't do everything. That's one of the reasons you need to focus on a niche. Find other "competitors" who have focused on different niches and strike a deal to do cooperative marketing.

For example, let's say you're a mortgage lender who focuses on FHA loans. You also get leads for construction loans, but you know that your business isn't well positioned to handle these types of loans. You can approach another lender that specializes in construction loans and strike a deal where you'll send them your leads for construction loans if they'll send you their leads for FHA loans. Although you're both technically competitors, by working together, you can each work your strengths and provide prospects an alternative that addresses your weaknesses.

How do you find the right competitors to approach? Use networking resources, or the Internet search engines to find those businesses that complement your weaknesses or strengths. As we discussed in Chapter 7, you can use Alexa (Alexa.com) to measure the success and traffic of a competitor's website. After you strike a deal, exchange website links and set them up so you can track the traffic that comes from their website. Then, you can thank them for the referrals you receive and they will know who linked to them through your website.

8. Joint ventures with affiliates

If you can do cooperative marketing with your competitors, why not also create joint ventures with the professionals you work with? As an experienced professional, you have a world

For a FREE 7-day course on "7 Steps To Building A Successful Marketing Plan," send an e-mail to ChipTips@ChipCummings.com

191

of information to share. But, your "value" doesn't stop there! You also know a host of other affiliated professionals: CPA's, lawyers, web designers, appraisers, surveyors, underwriters, title insurers, and many others. The simplest way to approach one of these affiliates is to work together on a free report that both your client bases can use.

Free reports (sometimes known as "white papers"), come from one of two perspectives: your personal experience or the knowledge of an affiliate experts (see Chapter 6 for a detailed look at putting reports together). Affiliates are always looking for joint venture opportunities that create a win-win solution for your clients. Reports can convey information, as well as demonstrate professional expertise, better than any other marketing tool. Again, listen to what your target market is hungry for — and then respond!

Another way you can leverage your affiliate relationships is through joint direct mailings. You can combine your mailing lists and share the cost of the mailing to deliver a coordinated message to both your customer lists. However, be aware of any regulatory restrictions on this form of advertising. For example, in the real estate business, the Real Estate Settlement Procedures Act (RESPA) restricts professionals in that industry to paying only for their portion of an advertisement. So, if you're working with a real estate professional and you are paying 50 percent of the bill for the mailing, make sure your material takes up 50 percent of the direct mail piece.

Using this method, you create that classic win/win scenario: you get to provide your customers with information from another recognized expert and they get new potential referrals from your customer base.

For a FREE 7-day course on "7 Steps To Building A Successful Marketing Plan," send an e-mail to ChipTips@ChipCummings.com

192

9. Yellow pages

Not every business can benefit from a telephone directory "yellow page" listing, but even a basic listing might be necessary for your business. There is a right way and wrong way to place a listing. First, you may need to list under different categories. Often the second category is less expensive. For example, if you provide a professional service you might want to obtain a listing under your company name *and* your personal name, depending on your industry. Second, use the ad not just to provide your contact information and what you do, but also to entice the reader to "do something" and contact you. This is where you can integrate several of the methods we've talked about up to this point.

For example, if your ad offers a free report, you can provide your website address (where they can fill out an online form), and an 800 number with a 24 hour recording that describes how they can get their report. This will increase response, and allow you to follow up with direct prospects!

10. Human Resource Departments

Perhaps your business provides a service that might be of interest to the employees of a major company. To access this rich source of leads, you have to build a relationship with the company's HR (Human Resource) department. This is similar to a joint venture with an affiliate. Here you propose to the HR department that you can set up an incentive program to provide benefits to their employees. The benefit to the HR department is twofold. First, they can add it as an employee benefit to increase the company's value in the eyes of its current employees. Second, it's another benefit the company can tout when recruiting new employees.

For a FREE 7-day course on "7 Steps To Building A Successful Marketing Plan," send an e-mail to ChipTips@ChipCummings.com

193

I once offered to do a free review of credit reports for employees of the U.S. Justice Department. I then offered to put together a free package of information about resources for employees relocating to the area. The package included information about how to get my free report on relocating. Did it pay off? Definitely. I captured numerous leads, and several of these employees went on to do mortgage loans with my company.

11. Business Cards

Business cards are your most important paper marketing tool. They are more than simply a vehicle for your contact information. They are, in fact, a "small billboard" for your business. They're the easiest marketing device to carry and distribute, so you want to take full advantage of this medium.

Here's how to get the most out of your business cards:

✦ **Use both sides.** Don't just rely on the contact information printed on the front. However, don't waste the reverse side of your business card. For example, in the mortgage business, many brokers use the backside of their business card to list the documents customers need to bring when they meet with the broker. This is not only not necessary, but I've found that this is intimidating and that most customers will opt to call a broker that doesn't include such a list. Instead, use the backside of your business card to offer a free report and list ways to get it (i.e. websites, 24 hour 800 number, e-mail, etc.).

✦ **Consider using your photo.** If you are in a professional service business that stresses individual attention, such as lawyers, doctors, real-estate, etc., a photo personalizes the business card. In other cases, a photo can still help

For a FREE 7-day course on "7 Steps To Building A Successful Marketing Plan," send an e-mail to ChipTips@ChipCummings.com

194

customers associate a face with the name, particularly if they meet you at an event where they collected many other business cards.

✦ **Reprint rather than mark up.** If you have to make a change to your card, have new ones printed as soon as possible. Avoid trying to salvage the incorrect cards and save money by scratching out the incorrect information and manually writing the new information. Hand-written corrections to one's own business card projects a poor image. Don't use computer generated cards — your cheapness will come shining through!

✦ **Put them where you need them.** Have you every rushed out of the house to go somewhere and realized that you forgot your business cards? Minimize the situations in which you are caught without extra business cards by placing stacks of cards in places you are most likely to have available when you when you leave your house. Here are some ideas for places to stage your business cards: wallet, car, briefcase, personal organizer, locker, and backpack.

12. Websites link swaps

Make sure you cross-link your website with appropriate affiliates. This can be as simple as a listing on the Resource page of each other's site or a pop-up ad. This is another great way to advertise the joint-venture report discussed earlier in this chapter.

Make sure you pick the right websites with which to exchange links (use the Alexa toolbar for researching these links). You will occasionally receive unsolicited invitations to swap links with websites that may have nothing to do with your industry or profession. Because the offer is free, this may be tempting, but I

For a FREE 7-day course on "7 Steps To Building A Successful Marketing Plan," send an e-mail to ChipTips@ChipCummings.com

195

suggest you avoid exchanging links with these "professional web link swappers" because they are typically "link farms" that will produce unqualified leads. Instead, if you are not sure where to find appropriate link partners, use the search techniques we addressed in Chapter 7 to find websites with the best traffic. Once you've identified a good candidate, you can use Alexa at Alexa.com to check the traffic and identify the owner. This usually includes contact information as well, or you can search the public record information at www.Whois.com for the contact information. I suggest you call the website owner and propose the link swap over the phone whenever possible or practical. This is a more personal approach than an e-mail and it gives you a chance to explain how the swap benefits both of you.

13. Direct mail

It's easy to think that direct mail is dead. After all, compared to e-mail, it's expensive and takes too long to print, fold, and mail. However, due to the saturation effect of e-mail advertising, direct mail is making a comeback. But, how you use it impacts your marketing effectiveness and your budget!

Like many of you, I get several hundred e-mails a day, and most of them get deleted automatically before ever seeing the inbox. For most of us, unless we recognize the sender or the "headline" (subject) of the e-mail, it usually just hits the electronic trashcan. When you couple that with the risk of viruses and "creative SPAM" that still sneak through and waste our time, paper direct mail starts to look good by comparison.

Old fashioned direct mail pieces can capture the customers' attention in a different context, leading to a longer impression time and greater impact and response than many e-mail marketing campaigns. But if you *combine* traditional direct mail with your online strategies, it can be pure magic!

For a FREE 7-day course on "7 Steps To Building A Successful Marketing Plan," send an e-mail to ChipTips@ChipCummings.com

196

If you use the right tool, you can manage your client databases and creatively extract filtered data to develop powerful e-mails, merged reports, and customized letters and marketing pieces. The goal is to drive as many "suspects" as you can into your electronic filtering system (website, auto responders, etc.) to generate quality prospects. Direct mail that is targeted and personalized will do just that.

For example, instead of sending a regular marketing piece to first-time homebuyers that lists my name, programs, and where to call, I will use a direct mail list in electronic format, then mail merge several of the fields to create personalized *greetings*, and customize the letter to them. I can crank off 5,000 customized marketing pieces in minutes! If you use the recipient's name 2 to 3 times and include their address, etc. in various parts of the marketing piece, it will have a different "feel" than a regular "junk-mail" piece.

Here's how to make direct mail work:

+ **Keep the message fairly short and simple.** You want them to contact you for more information, not read a boring sales novel!

+ **Drive the traffic to your website or autoresponder series.** Don't make your response trigger a "call to your office." They probably don't want to talk to you; they just want access to information.

+ **Offer useful information.** Use questions and curiosity to drive them to request free reports, website pages with authoritative information, or online calculators. Anonymous is good. People are more comfortable when they control the access and flow of information privately in their own timeframe. Make the piece information based, not an advertisement. People don't want to be sold — they will buy when they're ready.

For a FREE 7-day course on "7 Steps To Building A Successful Marketing Plan," send an e-mail to ChipTips@ChipCummings.com

197

Using these rules, do a joint-venture mailing with an affiliate to drive the traffic into your electronic marketing systems. For example, as we have previously discussed, if you were a mortgage lender, you could create a 2 to 4 page report entitled *"The 7 Most Common Tax Deductions Most People Miss"* by interviewing one of your local CPA's. Include his/her name as a resource, then prepare a letter or postcard that talks about the value of this free report. Then you could partner up with the CPA who wrote the report and a real estate agent to do a joint mailing piece to all your clients offering this free report through you. They can get it by filling out an electronic form on your website, by sending an e-mail, by calling your office, or by leaving a message. However they ask for it, you want to capture their information (name, e-mail address, postal address, phone number, etc.) for follow-up marketing. This is known as "opt-in" marketing, and now gives you permission to contact them without fear of violating any "do-not-call" or CAN-SPAM Act regulations.

This is only one example out of hundreds, but it again illustrates how a well thought-out marketing strategy can use both traditional and electronic methods of reaching your target market. You will produce the best results when you combine these strategies to capture customer information automatically.

14. Postcards

Postcards are particularly good for direct mail. Depending on the target market, I use creative postcards with an eye-catching photo and a simple message on the other side. There are several sizes of postcards to choose from including 4 by 6 inches, 5 ½ by 8 ½ inches, and 6 by 9 inches.

If you decide to use postcards, remember two simple rules. First, the picture side's only job is to get them to turn it over.

For a FREE 7-day course on "7 Steps To Building A Successful Marketing Plan," send an e-mail to ChipTips@ChipCummings.com

198

Second, the printed side should only contain one message theme with at least three response triggers (websites, 24 hour toll-free number, e-mail address, etc.) available to the reader.

There are four big advantages to postcards: First they are relatively inexpensive. Second, because of their size, they force you to keep your message short and simple. Third, you don't depend on the recipient to open anything — your message is immediately in front of them. Fourth, others will see your message as it makes its way to the recipient. A postcard may pass through the hands of many people at the recipient address or sit out in the open as it makes its way through a company's internal distribution system. This exposes your message to additional potential customers.

Postcards can be used for DRIP marketing campaigns, and could include recipes, home improvement tips, monthly specials, contests or giveaways, new products, service reminders, warranty information, or other special announcements.

15. Newspapers and magazines

Traditional advertising in newspapers and magazines can work if you do the right things. First, as with the other methods we've discussed, the ad should offer something (a free report, professional roundtable, special event, etc.) that induces your target audience to go to your website or call your 24 hour toll-free number.

Second, you must make sure there is some way to track the effectiveness of the ad. There are several ways you can do this. You can put a code in the ad that the interested party provides on your web form when they access your website. When they use your toll-free number to respond, the voice response system (like Information Now's 800service.com) can capture the caller's phone number. In addition to this, you can set your recorded message to

For a FREE 7-day course on "7 Steps To Building A Successful Marketing Plan," send an e-mail to ChipTips@ChipCummings.com

199

direct them to press a specific number corresponding to the offer you had in the ad. After hearing your message, the caller can leave a message. This not only allows you to track the effectiveness of the ad, but provides you the phone number of the caller. This is very useful, particularly if the caller started to leave a message from their cell phone but lost their signal before finishing. Since you have their number you can make a follow-up call.

Here's an example of how this might work. A real estate agent places an ad about a hot property in the newspaper and provides a toll-free number where people can call for additional information. Someone calls, punches in the correct code, hears your message, and either doesn't leave a message or is cut off in the middle of leaving a message. The system captured the caller's phone number and you call back to say "I don't know if you tried to leave a message and lost your cell phone signal, but I just wanted to get back in touch to make sure you got the information you were looking for." Using this twist on traditional advertising has turned an anonymous ad into a direct conversation with a qualified lead.

16. Niche periodicals

Niche periodicals include specialized magazines, newsletters, and journals. These publications focus on everything from cheerleaders to volunteer firefighters. They are great for narrowing your marketing to a particular target audience. There are two advantages to niche periodicals. First, ads are less expensive in niche periodicals. Second, the results you receive are much better because you are zeroing in on your target market.

To use this marketing method, you have to find the right periodical for your target audience. For example, if I'm trying to reach first time home buyers, I focus on auto trader publications and community newspapers — anything applicable to their

For a FREE 7-day course on "7 Steps To Building A Successful Marketing Plan," send an e-mail to ChipTips@ChipCummings.com

200

world. How do you find these publications? Talk to your customers. Find out what they read. Do a search on the Internet. Contact professional organizations that publish periodicals for professionals in your target market.

17. Open House Forums

Another way to create an event to draw your customers and prospects in and build your relationship is to offer an "inside view" of your business. You can do this by offering an open house or tour of your facilities.

Many non-profit and government agencies use this to get the public involved in what they do. For example, when I first moved into my neighborhood I saw in the paper that there was an open house for the local jail. Although I've never been in a jail, I was intrigued to learn about the atmosphere and facilities the jail maintained. It was a world that I normally would not see.

If you have a business that manufactures something, this can take the form of a tour. Large companies like Anheuser-Busch and Coca-Cola offer tours of their factories. If you aren't a manufacturer, you can combine an open house with the professional roundtable mentioned earlier in this chapter. This type of event gives your target audience a better perspective of what you do and provides an opportunity to learn more about your products and services in a non-threatening environment.

18. Recognition cards

Many businesses send holiday cards at Christmas time, but you can extend this idea to all kinds of other events or milestones. You can send cards for new years, fourth of July, birthdays, and anniversaries, just to name a few. For example, a real estate professional can send a card on the anniversary of when a customer moved into their home or commercial property.

For a FREE 7-day course on "7 Steps To Building A Successful Marketing Plan," send an e-mail to ChipTips@ChipCummings.com

201

To make this method more effective, combine the card with some gift like a discount coupon. To claim their discount, ask them to call a phone number or fill out a form on your website. This way you'll know who is responding to your recognition cards.

To put another technology twist on this idea, send an audio post card. In Chapter 10, I discussed how you can crate audio postcards using a service from www.Instant-Talking-Website.com. This provides a low cost way to deliver a personally recorded congratulatory message to your customers.

19. E-zines

We discussed creating your own e-zine in Chapter 9, but here we want to focus on e-zines where you can advertise your business. Look for e-zines that are complementary to your business or ones that target your audience.

There are several ways you can approach the e-zine publisher:

✦ **Buy a classified ad.** Many e-zines sell ad space in the e-zine. If they have a good sized distribution list that targets the right audience for your business, it may be worth purchasing a classified ad in the e-zine. Some e-zines will even offer this free, but you get what you pay for.

✦ **Write an article.** E-zine publishers are always looking for content. You can offer to provide a free article for their e-zine if you can include links to your website. I'll cover writing articles in more depth later in this chapter.

✦ **Ask for a link exchange.** See if the e-zine publisher is interested in exchanging links to your respective websites in each other's e-zines. You can make the same arguments as I discussed earlier in this chapter for websites link exchanges.

For a FREE 7-day course on "7 Steps To Building A Successful Marketing Plan," send an e-mail to ChipTips@ChipCummings.com

202

20. Promotional Parties

As I said earlier, it's important to touch your customers at least six times a year. However, when you accumulate a large number of customers, it becomes increasingly difficult to personally meet with each customer every year.

The answer is to create an event in which you can meet with a large number of customers all at once. For example, one time my office rented out the entire bleacher section to see a game with the local triple-A baseball team. We used direct mail, e-mail, and voice broadcast to invite our customers to the game. We asked them to contact us to reserve their tickets and join us for a picnic on a Sunday afternoon at the game. You can apply this same idea to hockey games, comedy clubs, horse races, etc.

This accomplished several things. First, it created an event where I and my staff could personally and directly interact with a large group of our customers in a non-threatening environment. Second, it provided a way for our customers to network with each other.

21. Hold messages and voicemail messages

More than likely, you use an automated answering system to take messages when you cannot answer the phone, or your system plays music when you have to put someone on hold. Rather than simply using your outgoing message to identify yourself or play music, put it to work directing traffic to your contact collection system.

While someone is on hold, you can play a message that says "Sorry you have to hold, but while you are waiting we wanted to let you know that you can get a free report: *The 7 Most Common Tax Deductions Most People Miss*. To get this report e-mailed to you, ask your representative when they come on the phone, or

For a FREE 7-day course on "7 Steps To Building A Successful Marketing Plan," send an e-mail to ChipTips@ChipCummings.com

203

go to our website at YourCompany.com." Use the same concept on your cell phone message as well!

22. Cassette tapes & CDs

Another way to distribute your information is as an audio cassette or CD. Not everyone likes to receive all their information in written form. For example, a busy professional may look for something to listen to in his or her car during long commutes. You can use this idea to distribute audio copies of your reports, professional roundtables, and teleconferences. Once you capture any of these recordings you can either create the cassettes and CD's yourself or use a copy house. The cost of blank cassettes and CDs is pretty low and there are plenty of inexpensive software programs to burn digital audio recordings on CDs.

One big advantage of these materials is that they are physical. They just seem to have more substance than a PDF attachment. Just make sure you use the same system to collect contact information from customers and prospects when they request your cassette or CD.

23. Brochures

Brochures can work for your business if you apply the same principle and offer valuable information to your target audience. Don't just talk about your business and its benefits. Include a reference to your free reports, newsletters, e-zines, cassettes, and CDs.

Some marketing experts advise businesses to move away from the traditional brochure and more towards media or information kits. However, there are times when a brochure can stand out more than a business card. For example, if you attend a professional organization or a chamber of commerce meeting, they may allow

For a FREE 7-day course on "7 Steps To Building A Successful Marketing Plan," send an e-mail to ChipTips@ChipCummings.com

204

you to display your marketing materials on a table. In this case, a brochure may stand out more than a stack of business cards. Also, when you meet a prospect at a meeting, providing a brochure may stand out more than just a business card because the cards might go unnoticed when the person you give it to dumps out a stack of them from their pocket after they go home.

24. Specialized mailing lists

You can leverage specialized direct mailing lists so you can market to very targeted customer base. Many professionals (doctors, lawyers, CPAs, etc.) have to register where they are licensed and you can purchase these lists. To avoid SPAM issues, you should use these lists only for your direct mail pieces.

Remember, never purchase e-mail lists. Those lists are quickly outdated and even if they claim to be "opt in" lists, it's hard to prove that the people in the list actually gave their permission to have their e-mail sold to outside parties.

25. Networking opportunities

Networking with professional organizations, your chamber of commerce, and clubs offers another way to personally spread your message. Odds are, there are plenty of professional organizations that have meetings close to where you live. In addition to networking opportunities, these organizations offer many other benefits including directory listings, training, publications, books, health plans, insurance, and discounts on office supplies and services.

In addition to networking in organizations where you expect to find your peers, attend events at organizations where you expect to find your clients. For example go to meetings of groups for doctors, CPAs, lawyers, executives, etc.

For a FREE 7-day course on "7 Steps To Building A Successful Marketing Plan," send an e-mail to ChipTips@ChipCummings.com

205

26. Giveaways

Well-known corporations do it, so why shouldn't you? As part of your marketing strategy, you can giveaway items to customers, affiliates, and prospects. This can include typical promotional items such as baseball caps, t-shirts, jackets, or tote bags pre-printed with your message. They can also be simple items you purchase and give away with your other marketing materials. For example, you can get a box of donuts for the office of your customers or affiliates and tape your business card to the box.

Whatever you choose for your giveaway, make sure you do more than just display your name and contact information. As with other methods in this list, ask the recipient to take action to get more goodies from you by directing them to a websites or toll-free number for free report, contest, or other incentive. This allows you to collect their contact information.

Recently, I attended an event that provided one of the best examples of this technique. The event sponsors gave away golf balls with the following message printed on them: "Oops! I lost a golf ball. I will pay you $5 to return it to me!" This was followed by their name and number. Even though it cost them $5 per response, the incentive was well worth the cost because they received good leads and built their prospect list (as well as some great stories!)

Many promotion printing companies allow you to purchase items in low quantities, so you don't have to tie up a lot of money in production of these items. One online vendor, Café Press (CafePress.com) offers over 50 items including T-shirts, jerseys, goodies, ceramic and stainless steel mugs, lunch boxes, and bags. There are no setup, pre-printing, or inventory fees because they only imprint an item when it is ordered.

For a FREE 7-day course on "7 Steps To Building A Successful Marketing Plan," send an e-mail to ChipTips@ChipCummings.com

206

When using this method, be careful that you do not run awry of legal restrictions on gift giving. For example, most levels of government prohibit vendors from giving gifts to government officials. In my industry, the Real Estate Settlement Procedures Act (RESPA) restricts individuals or companies from giving gifts to any person or entity that is in any way tied to the referral of business. Check to see if similar regulations apply to your industry.

27. Articles

Writing articles in a publication likely to be read by your target market establishes you as an expert in your field. Some publications pay for articles, but, when you consider the value of the article versus a paid advertisement in the same publication, it's worth it to write articles for free. The trick is to require that they let you include a resource box at the end of the article where you can offer your free report or free newsletter to drive readers to your websites or toll free number.

To prepare for an article proposal, first order a past edition of the publication and thoroughly read it, noticing not only the articles, but the kind of advertising they run. Find the copyright page where the publication usually lists the editorial staff and note the name of the editors. This page may even provide information for writers on how you can request the publication's Writer's Guidelines. This document will explain the proper procedure to submit an article idea to the publication. If they have one, call or write them requesting a copy. Then, propose your article by writing a query letter to the editor. In the query letter, you pitch your article idea and describe your qualifications to write the article.

What should you write about? How about a case history of how you solved a customer problem in a creative way? Write a review

For a FREE 7-day course on "7 Steps To Building A Successful Marketing Plan," send an e-mail to ChipTips@ChipCummings.com

207

of a new product or book applicable to your target market. Do a profile of an important industry leader. If you use your imagination, you'll be surprised how many ideas you'll come up with.

How do you find appropriate publications? Most professional organizations and associations publish industry specific publications that constantly need new content. Another useful resource is Writer's Market (WritersMarket.com.) They publish a book every year that lists periodicals and book publishers, but a quicker way to find appropriate publications is to subscribe to their online database. This is a searchable database of more than 5,600 writing markets in a wide range of niches.

If you do not enjoy writing, or are short on time, you can find many willing and able freelance writers waiting to help you with your project on sites such as www.elance.com!

28. TV/radio appearances

Similar to writing articles for publications you should seek to get on local radio or TV programs. The key is to pitch the radio or TV producer on a short (15-20 minute) subject that will appeal to their audience.

For example, I might say to a radio producer, "One of the things on people's minds this year is the tax implications of being a new home owner or how to get home equity loans at a decent rate. I know your listeners are interested in these subjects, because my office is getting requests for this information all the time. So, I'd like to offer you my time to do a quick interview to explain this to your audience and provide some value." In this example, I not only created an idea to provide valuable content to the producer, but I also provided a choice of subjects.

When you get on the show, be prepared to offer your free report or other incentive with your websites and toll-free phone number.

For a FREE 7-day course on "7 Steps To Building A Successful Marketing Plan," send an e-mail to ChipTips@ChipCummings.com

208

Also provide this information on a one page media sheet for the producer. This serves you in two ways. First, the station may continue to announce your free offer even after your interview is finished. Second, if a listener calls the station about your offer, they have this information handy to pass on to the listener.

29. Interview sessions

You don't need a real radio or cable show to be the subject of an interview. Find a tape recorder, a quite room, and a friend with a good voice. Write up a set of questions for your "interviewer" to ask that will bring out the high points of your business. One approach would be to create a "case study" about a client problem that you helped them solve.

Of course, it would be great if you can get a recognized leader in the market you are attacking. Try approaching the head of a professional organization or association in your target market. Perhaps you can strike a co-marketing deal with the interviewer where they can also market the recording to their customers. Depending on the stature of the interviewer, it might even be worth it to pay them to conduct the interview.

If you digitally record your interview or convert it to a digital format using your computer's sound card, you can use it in many ways. As we discussed in Chapter 10, you can put it on your websites, send it as an audio postcard, or burn it onto a CD.

30. Writing books

If you are willing to put in the time and you have a lot of patience, you can write a book about your field and perhaps interest a publisher. If you decide to tackle a book, be realistic. Writing a book is more time consuming and psychologically draining than any other type of writing you can imagine. You

For a FREE 7-day course on "7 Steps To Building A Successful Marketing Plan," send an e-mail to ChipTips@ChipCummings.com

209

can break the job down by drawing from a collection of your newsletters and reports.

To find publishers, purchase a copy of *The Writer's Market*, or better yet, subscribe to their publisher database at www.writersmarket.com. Using their database, you can find out which publishers are appropriate for your book proposal and their procedures for contacting them with your idea. Because publishers receive so many book proposals, you may want to enlist the services of an agent. A good agent can use his or her contacts to help you get your foot in the door. However, you have to sell a good agent on the idea of representing your book just as much as a publisher. Even if a publisher shows interest in your book, be prepared to wait a long time for an answer. Publishers can take anywhere from three months to a year to decide whether to publish your manuscript.

Another option is to self-publish. Benjamin Franklin, Walt Whitman, D.H. Lawrence, and Mark Twain all did it, so why not you? All these famous writes, self-published at least one of their books. If you just can't interest a publisher or agent in your manuscript and you're willing to invest additional time and money into the project, consider self-publishing your book.

Be prepared. When you go down the path of self-publishing, you are not just expressing yourself through the art of writing, but are creating an entirely new business. One that can add some additional revenue to your core business, but one that also has its own demands. As with your core business, you have to take time and money to market your book. Added to this, you have to manage the production, storage, and fulfillment (filling orders) of a physical product.

In addition to regular print publishing, there is the whole new world of e-publishing and Print on Demand (POD). E-publishing is the creation of a book in a purely electronic media. This can be

For a FREE 7-day course on "7 Steps To Building A Successful Marketing Plan," send an e-mail to ChipTips@ChipCummings.com

210

a book on CD or one you download from the Internet. There are several e-book formats but Adobe PDF is the most prevalent and easiest to produce. The biggest advantage of e-publishing is there are virtually no production costs.

POD publication uses a xerographic printing method to produce paper books from electronic files. Using this technology through a POD printer, you can produce books one at a time as they are ordered, or print very small batches of books. Although they cost more per book to produce, the main advantage of POD production is that you don't have to pay for and store a garage full of books before you sell them.

31. Customer membership clubs

One way you can maintain an ongoing relationship with your customers is to start a private membership club. This has become quite popular in the retail world. Airlines have their frequent flyer programs, Office Depot has their advantage program, and Subway has their Sub Club customer appreciation card, so it might make sense to have one yourself!

Bundle some set of services or discounts together and offer them to your past customers as part of a special club if they sign up to be a member. For example, for our mortgage customers we created an elite club that included free services for our customers when they stopped by our office. This included free use of our office copier, free notary services, discounts with area businesses, informational clinics, and seminars. We then required them to obtain a free renewal sticker each year so we could keep track of them! This is a great way to reward your loyal customers and keep them engaged with your business. To check out a pre-made membership site you can set up for yourself, visit www.MemberScript.com.

For a FREE 7-day course on "7 Steps To Building A Successful Marketing Plan," send an e-mail to ChipTips@ChipCummings.com

211

CHIP TIPS:

Here are your "personal road signs" from this Chapter:

1. Take traditional marketing methods and use your websites, auto responders, e-reports, and e-zines to add a technological twist.

2. Integrate your marketing messages by making sure that all your marketing efforts drive your prospects to give you their name and e-mail address.

For a FREE 7-day course on "7 Steps To Building A Successful Marketing Plan," send an e-mail to ChipTips@ChipCummings.com

212

Chapter 12

Playing Within The Rules

"Don't let what you can't do interfere with what you can do."

John Wooden

"**B**ut *everybody* does it" is not an excuse that will get you out of a speeding ticket from a police officer if you're caught going 90 MPH through a residential neighborhood. Nor will that excuse work if you get a call from the FTC or some other regulatory agency in response to an e-mail or website complaint or violation!

For a FREE 7-day course on "7 Steps To Building A Successful Marketing Plan," send an e-mail to ChipTips@ChipCummings.com

213

This chapter takes a look at some compliance issues surrounding the use of the various marketing concepts we have discussed. Of course, no book can substitute for personalized advice from a competent attorney or legal counsel. However, in this chapter I'll show you that, by instituting some standard policies and taking certain precautions, you can help avoid legal problems when implementing and using the marketing strategies described in this book.

CAN-SPAM Act

In response to a growing and overwhelming tide of complaints from people all over the country regarding the receipt of "unsolicited e-mail" (or SPAM) and other various obnoxious marketing techniques, the United States government passed the "Controlling the Assault of Non-Solicited Pornography and Marketing Act." This Act, also known as the "CAN-SPAM Act of 2003" became effective January 1, 2004. In typical government style, the "CAN" part of the Act's title does NOT mean that it is OK to SPAM! The primary purpose of the Act is to regulate unsolicited commercial email messages.

Unsolicited vs. Solicited commercial e-mail

Commercial e-mail is any electronic message whose primary purpose is the commercial advertisement or promotion of a product or service, including content on an internet website, operated for a commercial purpose. Unsolicited e-mail is any e-mail that you receive without your request, from a party with which you had no previous relationship. Solicited e-mail is any e-mail you receive from a party with which you requested, or "opted-in," to receive electronic correspondence. The Act does not prohibit the sending of unsolicited commercial email, it only regulates how you send any commercial e-mail, both unsolicited and solicited.

For a FREE 7-day course on "7 Steps To Building A Successful Marketing Plan," send an e-mail to ChipTips@ChipCummings.com

214

Requirements

To assist you, here are some of the basic requirements to comply with the CAN-SPAM act:

1. In the "From" line of your e-mail message, you must provide an accurate, non-fraudulent name and return e-mail address. In other words, if someone clicks "Reply," the message they send must go to a real e-mail address.

2. The "Subject" line of your message must accurately represent the content contained in the body of email and, if applicable, you must label any sexually-oriented messages. You cannot try to trick someone by making the message look like it's from their mother or some other similar deception. If you are sending unsolicited e-mail, you must include some indication that the message is an advertisement. The clearest way to do this is to include "Advertisement" or "ADV" in the subject line. However, if you are sending solicited (i.e. opt-in) e-mail, you do not have to identify it as an advertisement.

3. You must include an actual postal address in the body of the e-mail. It is acceptable to include a P.O. Box, but it must be a legitimate postal address.

4. You must provide an easy "opt-out" procedure in the body of the e-mail message. After someone opts-out, you have a 10-day grace period to remove that person's e-mail address from your lists.

Penalties

The penalties for violations of the CAN-SPAM Act are quite serious, and vary based upon the type of violation. Pursuant to Section 5 of the Act, in addition to ordering an injunction against your business, the Federal Trade Commission (FTC) can level

For a FREE 7-day course on "7 Steps To Building A Successful Marketing Plan," send an e-mail to ChipTips@ChipCummings.com

215

fines for certain violations that cost $250 for each e-mail address that was affected by the violation. Obviously, this can get real expensive, real fast!

State and international compliance

The CAN-SPAM Act supersedes all state laws that deal with commercial electronic messages. Outside the U.S., there are laws of reciprocity in most industrial countries. While still somewhat untested and unclear as to the possible ramifications, this means that under certain situations, the FTC may still be able to enforce elements of the Act, even if the messages originate in other countries.

"Do Not Call" Lists

On October 1, 2003, the national "Do Not Call/Do Not Fax" registry went into effect. The Federal government created the national registry to make it easier and more efficient for consumers to stop getting telemarketing calls that they don't want.

The Registry applies to any business with a plan, program or campaign to sell goods or services through interstate phone calls. This includes telemarketers who solicit consumers on behalf of third party sellers and sellers who provide, offer to provide, or arrange to provide goods or services to consumers in exchange for payment. In other words, just about everybody!

Requirements

The regulations require telemarketers (or any company calling consumers) to search the registry at least every three months and eliminate any phone numbers of registered consumers from their call lists.

For a FREE 7-day course on "7 Steps To Building A Successful Marketing Plan," send an e-mail to ChipTips@ChipCummings.com

216

However, you may call a consumer with whom you have an established business relationship, for up to 18 months after the consumer's last purchase, delivery, or payment — even if that person's number is on the National Do Not Call Registry. You can also call a consumer for up to three months after the consumer makes an inquiry or submits an application to your company.

If a consumer asks a company not to call, the company may not telephone that consumer for any marketing purpose, even if there is an established business relationship. As a matter of fact, you may not call a consumer at all (regardless of whether the consumer's number is on the registry), if the consumer has asked to be put on the company's own do not call list.

For your protection as a business owner or professional salesperson, I strongly suggest that you maintain a "Do Not Call" list of your own for internal purposes. Make sure that everyone in your company has access to the list, and knows the proper procedures for "checking it twice" before making any outbound marketing calls — even to your existing client base.

To make it easier to communicate efficiently with your customer base, I recommend that you maintain an e-mail database list for marketing purposes. Obtain a customer's e-mail address early during the sales process as an "opt-in" for communications, e-zines, announcements, updates, notices, specials, etc. They will have the option of "opting out" of the list later if they decide to, but you can contact them easier, less expensively, and with fewer potential problems using this technique.

Penalties

The penalties for violating the "Do Not Call" list regulations are even steeper than with the CAN-SPAN act. Violators are subject to a fine of up to $11,000 per violation, as well as

For a FREE 7-day course on "7 Steps To Building A Successful Marketing Plan," send an e-mail to ChipTips@ChipCummings.com

217

injunctions to prevent further violations. They are serious about cracking down on violators, as several large fines have already been handed down.

Accessing the list

For compliance purposes, the FTC provides a dedicated, fully automated, secure website at www.Telemarketing.donotcall.gov. The first time you access the system, you have to provide some identifying information, such as organization name and address, authorized representative, and the representative's telephone number and email address. If you are accessing the registry on behalf of a client-seller, you may need to identify the client(s).

The only consumer information that you can access in the list is a registrant's telephone number. The registry sorts the list by consumer area code and phone number, and you will have to pay an annual fee to use the list based on the number of area codes you access. On subsequent visits to the Do Not Call Registry website, you can download either a complete updated list of numbers from selected area codes or a more limited list that shows additions or deletions since the last download.

To ADD your own personal number to the list, you can go to www.DoNotCall.gov. Here you can list your personal residence and/or cellular telephone numbers. The registration is good for five years, then needs to be renewed.

What you should do

DON'T PANIC! You can run an efficient business and still stay within ethical and government guidelines by instituting some basic policies. This includes policies for commercial electronic messages, opt-in procedures, third-party advertising, websites policies, and database management.

For a FREE 7-day course on "7 Steps To Building A Successful Marketing Plan," send an e-mail to ChipTips@ChipCummings.com

218

Electronic messages

Here's what you should do make sure you comply with the CAN-SPAM Act:

1. Use a company that provides professional list management, and warrants the list's accuracy and timeliness (such as www.SimpleAutoresponders.com). When you send your commercial e-mails through such a list management service, they will automatically make sure your messages comply with key provisions of the CAN-SPAM Act. For example, they can automatically insert the opt-out link and your physical address at the bottom of your messages, as well as maintain your opt-in list. This way, if necessary, you can prove when someone joined your list.

2. Create an "opt-in strategy." If you've been paying attention to what I've been saying in other chapters of this book, you already have an opt-in strategy, using an offer for free reports and web forms to get your customer's permission to engage in a dialog with them. This is known as "Permission-based Marketing."

3. Include a real name and return address. You don't have to use your personal e-mail address, but don't try to hide behind a bogus return e-mail address. Set up an e-mail address specifically for this purpose, such as info@yourcompany.com or CustomerService@yourcompany.com. Besides, you want to engage in a two-way relationship with your customers — not alienate them!

4. Clearly and conspicuously label your message in the "Subject" line. Make sure the subject line accurately represents the content of the body of your email. However, you can be creative with the subject line to get the recipient to open it. For

For a FREE 7-day course on "7 Steps To Building A Successful Marketing Plan," send an e-mail to ChipTips@ChipCummings.com

219

example, with solicited e-mail, you can put something like "Len, I almost forgot..." or "Judy: Important and urgent."

5. If it IS an unsolicited message, make sure you make it clear that it is advertising. Put "ADV" or "Advertising" in the subject line.

6. Include your postal address in the body of the e-mail. To protect your own privacy, you can use a P.O. Box., but it must be a "real" address.

7. Develop and enforce an organization-wide "opt-out" process. Provide an easy (preferably one-step) opt-out procedure and make sure the "unsubscribe" link works. When someone opts-out, make sure you get them off **all** your electronic mailing lists. Remember, you have a 10 day grace period to get someone off your list. It's probably a good idea to also maintain a purge list to prevent them from re-appearing on the list. If you use a company that provides professional list management, they will do this for you. Make sure you know their procedures and policies though, as you can't dump off your legal responsibilities to them — you're still liable!

8. Make sure your staff and employees know and enforce the regulations. All it takes is one mistake from one employee to create a problem, so make sure your staff is trained in the proper procedures.

Opt-in procedures

Per the CAN-SPAM Act, a customer "opts-in" when he or she "expressly [consents] to receive the message, either in response to a clear and conspicuous request for such consent or at the recipient's own initiative." Other terms for establishing an "opt-in" is an affirmative consent, permission marketing, or direct consent. For example, at many of my presentations, I offer a free

For a FREE 7-day course on "7 Steps To Building A Successful Marketing Plan," send an e-mail to ChipTips@ChipCummings.com

220

report or gift to the people in attendance. When they provide a business card or reply card in response to the offer, they have "opted-in" to my list!

The CAN-SPAM Act reinforces the benefits of using an opt-in policy for your commercial messages. Since the Act does not require you to identify solicited messages as advertising, this clearly gives an advantage to those organizations that send only to "opt-in" lists. So, as I've covered elsewhere in this book, make sure you build your list by getting people to send an e-mail request or filling out a web form on your websites.

One important question that remains, is whether to use a "single" or a "double" opt-in system. In a double-opt in system, you send a follow-up message to the e-mail address that the customer provided, asking them to click on a link that will confirm their decision to opt-in to your list. The advantage to this system is that you make sure that someone other than the customer did not "volunteer" the customer for the list without their consent. It also eliminates opt-ins from automated reply systems. The disadvantage to this system is that 50% or more of the people receiving a request to double opt-in do not respond, so as a result they are dropped from your list. The list that you DO end up with in a double opt-in system however, is very valuable and HIGHLY responsive!

Keep in mind that the CAN-SPAM Act **does not** require a double opt-in before you can send solicited e-mail. This means you can still use a single opt-in system to collect names and e-mail addresses for solicited e-mails (i.e. those e-mails that do not require you to identify them as advertising in the Subject line). I recommend using a single opt-in system for most applications. Double opt-in systems are very useful for specialized promotions, highly targeted response lists, bonus attachments, and similar situations. So, you will have to decide whether the

For a FREE 7-day course on "7 Steps To Building A Successful Marketing Plan," send an e-mail to ChipTips@ChipCummings.com

221

need to add an extra level of security by using a double opt-in system outweighs the decline in confirmed opt-ins when building your list.

Third-party advertising

As I discussed in Chapter 11, one marketing strategy that will help you build a permission-based list quickly, is to engage in joint direct mailings with other affiliate partners where you might promote a third party product or service to your list. As far as the CAN-SPAM act is concerned, one potential problem with this strategy is that if a recipient decides to opt-out, they will only be removed from your list not the third party's list. Even though you haven't directly shared your list with the third party, the recipient may have also registered with them and when they opted-out of your list they *think* they've also opted out of the third party's list. So, when the third party sends them their own, seemingly solicited, e-mail, the recipient can get angry and file a complaint against the third party.

A possible way to avoid this kind of problem is to include two opt-out options at the bottom of your message. The first is for your list and the second is for the third party list. Although it presents a two-step process for the recipient, at least they are alerted to the fact that you don't control the third party's list.

Websites legal documents

Websites are available to anyone on the planet that has access to an Internet connection. As such, there are some essential documents that you should have on your websites to protect you from potential legal hassles. These items include terms of use and disclaimers, a privacy policy, and possibly an affiliate agreement. Talk to a good Internet attorney to discuss your specific needs and requirements. Here are a few you will want to consider:

For a FREE 7-day course on "7 Steps To Building A Successful Marketing Plan," send an e-mail to ChipTips@ChipCummings.com

222

Terms of use and disclaimers

You should post a Terms of Use agreement on your websites that establishes the terms and conditions for use of your site. It's particularly important if your site sells or licenses software, content, services, or physical goods. It is a key agreement that should coordinate with your privacy policy, sales agreements, and license agreements. This manages the legal risks of operating an e-commerce business, including reliance issues (accuracy of links and professional advice), copyright and trademark infringement, warranty liability, damage exposure, consumer rights liability, risk of loss, litigation and dispute resolution, foreign law, and choice of forum, and privacy rights exposure. If you sell or license software through your websites, you should also have clauses that protect you in the event you, or any of your affiliates accidentally pass on a virus through your software to your customers.

It is beyond the scope of this book to detail all the ways you can write such an agreement, but one tool that provides pre-written legal documents for your websites is AutoWebLaw Pro (AutoWebLaw.com). Don't adopt any legal disclosures or documents on or through your site without discussing them with your attorney.

Privacy Policy

As I've emphasized throughout this book, I believe you should never, ever, sell, lend, trade, or license your customer list to any third party. Make sure you communicate this and other privacy issues through a Privacy Policy posted (or linked) through every page on your website. Actually, your privacy policy can also act as a way to educate your customer, especially since people who click on a link to read the privacy policy are typically highly motivated customers.

For a FREE 7-day course on "7 Steps To Building A Successful Marketing Plan," send an e-mail to ChipTips@ChipCummings.com

223

If your website collects or monitors information from visitors by any means, including web forms, cookies, referrer data, IP addresses, and/or system information, you need to have a written privacy policy. Also, even if you only expect adults to be interested in your site, your privacy policy should also include a children's privacy clause that protects you against use of your site by minors or under-aged users.

If you are not sure how to word your privacy policy, get help from your attorney or get pre-written privacy policy documents from a vendor like www.AutoWebLaw.com.

Affiliate program agreement

Affiliate partners are a great way to expand your business. If you use registered affiliates as your extended sales force however, you should have an affiliate agreement. An affiliate agreement protects you from actions that your affiliate may take that will violate the CAN-SPAM Act or other regulations when selling your product or services.

You should have an affiliate agreement that sets forth the terms and conditions upon which an affiliate markets for you. The agreement should stress that the affiliate is not your employee and that they are an independent business. Your agreement should stress that the affiliate must comply with all government rules and regulations. Make sure you include a check box on their sign up form that indicates that they read the agreement and consent to its rules. If you institute any amendments to the agreement, make sure you send the changes to all the affiliates when they take effect. This covers you in case you have to amend your agreement to keep up with government changes to regulations such as the CAN-SPAM Act.

For a FREE 7-day course on "7 Steps To Building A Successful Marketing Plan," send an e-mail to ChipTips@ChipCummings.com

224

Database Management

Managing your database correctly is critical. Earlier in this book, I talked about splitting your customers into three categories: future, present, and past. Make sure that when someone opts-out of a commercial mailing from your organization, that you update all your lists — both online and offline. For example, if you use a list manager service (such as www.SimpleAutoresponders.com), they will automatically handle opt-outs from that list, but you may still have customer e-mail addresses on your in-house e-mail system, so make sure you also mark that list so you don't send any commercial e-mails using that system.

Technology and the marketing strategies that I use and teach people to implement, are a very powerful way to attract and capturing new customers, while significantly impacting your profits. Even though it's a lot of fun to see your Prospect and Customer lists grow, it's equally important to do it the right way! DON'T try to short-cut the process and save a few bucks by trying to do it yourself — it's not worth it. You have better things to do, and a dollar spent in prevention and professional database management could save you thousands in the long run — trust me!

For a FREE 7-day course on "7 Steps To Building A Successful Marketing Plan," send an e-mail to ChipTips@ChipCummings.com

225

CHIP TIPS:

Here are your "personal road signs" from this Chapter:

1. The CAN-SPAM Act of 2003 became effective January 1, 2004. The rules for handling commercial solicited vs. unsolicited e-mail are slightly different. If you send unsolicited e-mail, the subject line must make it obvious that the message is advertising. The easiest way to do this is to include the word "Advertisement" or "ADV" in the subject line. When you send solicited e-mail, you do not have to indicate that it is advertising in the subject line.

2. Other rules of the CAN-SPAM act require you to include the following:

    a) A valid return e-mail address

    b) A Postal address in the body of the message, and

    c) An easy way for the recipient to opt-out.

3. The Do Not Call Registry requires you to remove the phone number of any consumer listed in the Registry from your telemarketing list, unless you have an established business relationship. You can access the official list from the FTC Register websites at telemarketing.donotcall.gov.

4. Make sure your staff and employees know your policies and internally enforce the regulations.

5. Make sure your website has the following legal documents: terms of use, privacy policy, and affiliate program agreement.

For a FREE 7-day course on "7 Steps To Building A Successful Marketing Plan," send an e-mail to ChipTips@ChipCummings.com

226

Chapter 13

The Art and Science of Listening

*"The successful people I've known are the ones
who do more listening than talking."*
Bernard M. Baruch

H ave you ever gotten into your car on your way to work, then once you are there — wondered exactly how you got there? Repetition creates habits, which become engrained into our subconscious. You are able to drive to work on "auto-pilot" because it has become routine, having to react only to changes or distractions. Seasoned drivers are always aware of their surroundings, reacting with instinct, but allowing their "auto-pilot" to control routine functions. Experience and repetition turn conscious actions into unconscious ones. Nothing takes the place of experience.

Listening also takes experience. The skill of listening is more than just hearing words. It means comprehending verbal as well as non-verbal language, emotions, movements, gestures, habits and responses. Becoming really good at listening takes a lot of time, patience and study. But as with anything else, the more you practice, the better you get!

For a FREE 7-day course on "7 Steps To Building A Successful Marketing Plan," send an e-mail to ChipTips@ChipCummings.com

227

The Art of Listening

The art of listening revolves around one of the themes expressed in the title of this book. In other words **start listening!** A Top Producer knows how to ask the right questions, determine the customer's needs, select potential solutions, and boil their presentation down to just two or three of the best solutions matching the customer's needs. Much of the art of listening comes down to asking the right questions. To help you practice this, here are nine rules that will prepare you to ask the right questions and get quality answers:

1. **Ask "open-ended" questions.** Avoid asking questions that the customer can only answer with one word, or with a simple "yes" or "no" response. You will generally not get enough information from these kinds of questions to determine the customer's needs. Instead ask open-ended questions that require the customer to provide precious details. For example, rather than ask my customer "Are you thinking of buying a house?" I'll ask "What is your ideal house?" or "What is your ideal neighborhood?"

2. **Don't confuse the customer with too many options.** A confused mind always says "no." Although there may be a hundred potential solutions to the customer's problem, you don't want to list them all for the customer. Part of the reason that customers come to you, and the added value you provide is your ability to listen, filter the options, and present the best two or three solutions. In this capacity, you are acting as a trusted advisor, saving the customer loads of time that they would have to spend weighing each option and eliminating the impractical solutions. This is part of your "Personal Value".

3. **Ask past customers about their experience.** Don't simply ask if they experienced a good transaction. Ask for

For a FREE 7-day course on "7 Steps To Building A Successful Marketing Plan," send an e-mail to ChipTips@ChipCummings.com

228

specifics. Pick one or two customers a month and personally call them and ask them for detailed feedback. For example, you can ask, "When you first came to us, what were your impressions? When you first contacted us, what was that like? Was the final result what you expected? Was it more? Was it less? Did we fulfill all your expectations? If you were to go through the process again, what would you like to experience differently?" When you get responses, don't try to defend, justify or explain your actions. Just *listen* and absorb the information.

4. **Gauge non-verbal customer reactions.** When you ask customers questions, they don't always tell you what they think. For example, when you ask someone for their opinion about your website, brochure, or audio message over the phone, they might not be able to communicate everything through words alone. So, interview a few customers in person so you can see their reactions to your marketing materials.

5. **Interview non-interested parties.** Talk to parties about your business operations that are not associated with your business as a customer, prospect, or employee. The feedback you get from this exercise will act as a reality check on the focus and design of your website and marketing materials. Here are some questions you can ask: "What would you do when you go to our website or read our brochure. What is the perceived main focus? What are you inclined to do when you visit our website or read our marketing materials? What about these materials peaked your interest or turned you off?"

6. **Interview yourself.** Analyze your strengths and weaknesses. Ask yourself "If you were your competition, what would you do to beat yourself in the marketplace?"

For a FREE 7-day course on "7 Steps To Building A Successful Marketing Plan," send an e-mail to ChipTips@ChipCummings.com

229

7. **Map out the ideal customer experience.** After you ask the above questions, you can identify and document the ideal customer experience. In Chapter 6, I covered how to design your customer's websites experience. Here I'm asking you to map out the ideal *total* customer experience from the point of awareness to the point of purchase and beyond. You not only want to identify what the ideal customer experience should be, but what to do if something derails that experience. Once you identify the ideal customer experience, document it and make sure that every member of your team knows and buys into delivering that experience. This way, if something goes wrong, everyone in your organization knows what they need to do to fix the problem.

8. **Refer to the customer by name.** As you follow your plan to deliver an outstanding customer experience, make sure you address the customer by name every chance you get. You can do this electronically by including their name in the Subject line and body of the message. When you work with a customer in person, make sure you interject their name throughout your presentation to keep them from tuning you out.

9. **Ask for testimonials.** Prepare your customer to give you a testimonial by asking for it early in the transaction. When you start dealing with them, ask "If I can deliver everything you need, will you provide me with a testimonial I can provide to other customers?" When they agree to give you a testimonial, make sure you get as colorful and detailed a testimonial as possible. "I had a great experience" or "The service was good" is too generic. Try to get them to explain in their own words how you solved their problem and what it meant to them. A written testimonial is good. A recorded

For a FREE 7-day course on "7 Steps To Building A Successful Marketing Plan," send an e-mail to ChipTips@ChipCummings.com

230

audio testimonial is better. See if they will record their testimonial for playback on your websites. Testimonials will also provide insight as to where your strengths lie, and careful listening will reveal UVP benefits.

The Science of Listening

In The Art of Listening, you ask the important questions to build your marketing materials and map out the ideal customer experience. In the Science of Listening, you track patterns and results to see how well your marketing messages are working. You want to track consistent predictability by measuring how customers react to your website, e-mail autoresponders, and every other marketing piece you have in place.

Tracking

You must be able to track where you are generating the most interest from your target market from each of your marketing methods. This way you can figure out which ones are working and which ones you should drop. So, you need a logical and consistent system for tracking any of your marketing methods. Here are some ideas:

1. **Use multiple phone numbers.** If you place ads in different publications, you need a way to track which ad is working best. There are several ways to accomplish this. For example, you can use different phone numbers for people to call. Then you can track results based on the number of calls you get from each number. Another method is to include a code in the ad by telling the customer to "Ask for department X" where "X" is a letter you designate for a particular publication. Other systems, such as Information

For a FREE 7-day course on "7 Steps To Building A Successful Marketing Plan," send an e-mail to ChipTips@ChipCummings.com

231

Now's call capture system (www.800service.com) will allow you to have multiple extensions set up and programmed for different ads and clients.

2. **Use different domain names.** You can register multiple domain names that all forward to your website or a specific web page such as an autoresponder sign-up page. Then, you can use these domain name variations in your marketing materials and electronically track how people arrive at your websites. You can also use this method to see which domain names attract the most traffic through search engines, or use separate domains for individual ads in newspapers, periodicals, flyers, or pay-per-click services such as Google's AdWords.

3. **Use the Alexa toolbar.** Elsewhere in this book, I told you about the Alexa toolbar — a great free tool that ranks all of the websites on the Internet. Go to Alexa.com and make sure you download this tool and use it to periodically track your website ranking. This tool provides several benefits. First, you can use it to track your own site ranking to see if your marketing efforts are paying off. Second, you can use it to find related websites with even better traffic that you can approach to exchange site links. Third, you can use it to regularly track the rankings of your closest competitors and track the links that go in and out of their website!

4. **Monitor traffic reports.** Check to see if your website host provides statistics about visitors to your website. Key statistics that you want to monitor include number of visitors, number of page views, and keywords that they used to find your site. If your host does not provide easy to read reports, you can use the free software available at webalizer.com to read standard server log files provided by your host.

For a FREE 7-day course on "7 Steps To Building A Successful Marketing Plan," send an e-mail to ChipTips@ChipCummings.com

232

5. **Track affiliate connections.** Apply the same tracking techniques to your affiliates. Find out which links on their websites are drawing the most traffic. Adjust your pitch to emphasize those affiliates or co-marketing programs that bring you the most prospects, and consider dropping those that don't measure up.

Listening To YOUR Marketing

One of the most productive exercises that I do with consulting clients, is to have them evaluate what their marketing is telling them. Take some time to go through these steps, and hear what your marketing materials are saying about you:

1. Make sure that you have completed the exercises in Chapter 4 in developing your UVP and seven-second statement.

2. Gather up every piece of marketing material about you and your company (printed, audio, pictures, yellow pages ads, etc.) that you can find — old and new.

3. Evaluate each marketing piece — does is contain or exhibit your UVP? What is the marketing piece asking the customer to do? Are there multiple or conflicting themes or messages that might confuse a Prospect? Does the message use simple easy-to-understand language? Does the message contain enough information to get the Prospect to do what it is you want them to do? What is the value provided to the Prospect? Are their multiple response triggers for them to react to? Does it clearly fit the target market? Write down all your answers for each marketing piece.

4. Find two previous customers or Prospects that fit the target market group, and ask them the same questions from above.

For a FREE 7-day course on "7 Steps To Building A Successful Marketing Plan," send an e-mail to ChipTips@ChipCummings.com

233

Do their answers match yours? Listen to their answers carefully, then redesign each marketing piece until it "speaks" clearly to the Prospects in the target market group.

Testing

In addition to tracking and monitoring the success (or failure) of your marketing efforts, you should be constantly testing different versions of your marketing communications. Here are just a few of the items you can test:

1. **Headlines.** The headline for e-mail messages, auto responder messages, and direct mail is the most important element of those marketing campaigns. Create a few different versions of your headline and split your recipient list to test which ones get the best response. Use as many ACTION words as possible!

2. **Websites design.** When someone types in the URL for your websites, you can forward the traffic to any one of several versions of your site. Create different versions of your websites to test elements such as websites colors, page position (left, center, etc.), and response triggers (i.e. offers for free reports, consultations, etc.)

3. **Pop ups.** Many pop up managers offer the ability to rotate different pop up messages. This allows you to test the text, position, and exit path of a pop up to see which one works best.

4. **Colors.** Test a variety of color themes to see if the reaction changes. The best colors to use are green, blue and red. The worst colors are usually yellow, orange, brown, and pink.

5. **Timing.** Vary the timing of your messages to see if the response changes. Business to business messages should not

For a FREE 7-day course on "7 Steps To Building A Successful Marketing Plan," send an e-mail to ChipTips@ChipCummings.com

234

be tested on a Friday, or over the weekend. Allow at least 2 days between autoresponder messages (as a general rule) to allow people to receive and open the message. More time should be allotted for messages that contain detailed information or attached reports. For certain industries, different times of the day might make it impossible for certain Prospects to react to the message.

6. **Delivery Methods.** I will constantly test various forms of delivery, including e-mail messages, HTML formats, web page links, PDF's, audio postcards, as well as numerous text and scripts.

Only test up to two variances at any given time, and let the test run long enough to give you strong statistical results. Take the "winner" of the test, then split test it with another variable and repeat this approach until you are satisfied that you are experiencing optimal results. Then re-test your results at least 1-2 times per year to identify possible market and consumer changes and trends.

This process will help you to remain focused on the value you bring to your Prospects and Customers, and stay ahead of the market and competition. Do not participate in "name recognition" type marketing strategies. Only implement strategies where you can directly measure the results. This will not only produce direct profits, but will build name recognition at the same time!

For a FREE 7-day course on "7 Steps To Building A Successful Marketing Plan," send an e-mail to ChipTips@ChipCummings.com

235

CHIP TIPS:

Here are your "personal road signs" from this Chapter:

1. Remember, your marketing message has no power in and of itself. The power is in the art of listening!

2. By mastering the art of listening, you will not only find out what your customers want today, but also stay ahead of customer trends coming down the road.

3. As you track, test, and perfect your marketing methods, remember that you cannot please everyone. For example, you may get some conflicting design suggestions for your websites. Some people may prefer one color and others a different color. If you try to please everyone, you will succeed in being so generic and mediocre that you won't please anyone. How do you decide who's right? Design your message around the needs of your ideal customer; the one who you want to become an evangelist for your business. This may only be 10 percent of your customer base, but that 10 percent will help bring in the other 90 percent.

4. Take the time to analyze each marketing piece that you have to determine the direct value to the target market. Don't implement a marketing strategy for "name recognition" purposes.

For a FREE 7-day course on "7 Steps To Building A Successful Marketing Plan," send an e-mail to ChipTips@ChipCummings.com

236

Chapter 14

___

Your Personal Roadmap To Success

"The road to success is always under construction."

Anonymous

"You can't do everything at once, but you can do SOMETHING at once."

Chip Cummings

Throughout this book, I've shared many different strategies that I have personally used (and continue to use), as well as several which are used by many different Top Producers from around the world. All the strategies in the world are meaningless, unless you make a conscious decision to start implementing them yourself.

I have one more secret to share with you — it won't happen overnight. The formulas shared over the past 13 chapters DO work, but you have to start one step at a time, and give it a little time. Let's get started by building your own personal "roadmap to success".

___

For a FREE 7-day course on "7 Steps To Building A Successful Marketing Plan," send an e-mail to ChipTips@ChipCummings.com

237

Seven Steps to E-Success

So, what do you do first thing tomorrow morning? Well, while each of these steps encompasses a broad range of tasks (which can vary depending on your industry and niche), here are seven steps which will help you maximize your success in designing and implementing your marketing strategies, including your website, autoresponder series, e-mails, and reports.

For a FREE 7-day course on "7 Steps To Building A Successful Marketing Plan," send an e-mail to ChipTips@ChipCummings.com

238

1. **Do your research.**

   a. **Do market research.** Understand what your market wants, where they are spending their time and money presently, and which mediums are reaching them the best. Make sure you understand their problems so you can develop the appropriate product/service solutions. Are they reacting differently or using other types of solutions than they were six, twelve or twenty-four months ago?

   b. **Research the competition.** Look at your competition. Understand how they're getting their business. Where are they located? What are they doing? What is their market identity, and how are they positioning *their* value?

   c. **Choose the right products for the market.** ASK QUESTIONS to find out what problem(s) plague your niche, and formulate your services to offer a direct solution. Since consumers are bombarded with so many choices, being "all things to all people" isn't appealing. So, Specialize to Profitize! Know your competitors' products and how they compare to your own.

   d. **Develop your UVP and 7-second statement.** In less than seven seconds, you must be able to define what value you represent to Prospects in your particular industry. Answer these three questions: What industry are you in? What specialty within that industry are you targeting? What problem is my niche trying to solve?

2. **Build The Foundation.**

   a. **Register domain names.** When setting up your domain name, make it simple and memorable. Stick with dot-com names for main websites. Customers will not check other

For a FREE 7-day course on "7 Steps To Building A Successful Marketing Plan," send an e-mail to ChipTips@ChipCummings.com

239

extensions such as .biz, .net, .org, etc. Anticipate customer misspellings of your domain name and reserve those versions also. Use .net or other extensions for split testing, market extensions, or PPC routing.

b. **Choose a host that you control.** Make sure that regardless of the provider you choose to host your websites, that you maintain control over the design of at least the entry page of the website. Avoid just using fixed templates that might make your websites look like others, but use templates for the "back room" operations.

c. **Design the web experience.** Visit your competitors' websites. Make sure visitors to your website know they found the right place and can get to what they want in seven seconds or less. Test your websites with an eight year old to see if it is simple to navigate. Test it on several non-affiliated individuals, and test each click to make sure it works smoothly and quickly.

d. **Create Personal Value.** Create free reports, tele-conferences, affiliate partners and joint ventures with similar or related quality businesses. Make sure you are establishing yourself as an expert in your industry.

3. **Write Killer Copy.**

a. **Write your own copy or hire a copywriter.** You only get a short time to capture a prospect's attention. They need to know that it's the right site, and that you have what they came to find.

b. **Use action words.** Use verbs rather than adjectives because they make people react a greater percentage of the time.

For a FREE 7-day course on "7 Steps To Building A Successful Marketing Plan," send an e-mail to ChipTips@ChipCummings.com

240

c. **Have a specific "Call To Action."** Make it easy for your customers and prospect to give you their contact information by offering something for free. Include phrases like "Click here to get this free report." However, don't try to sell your prospects something right away. Remember, you don't get married on the first date!

d. **Keep one thought per web page.** Treat each page like a sales letter that focuses like a laser beam on a specific subject.

e. **Remove any objections.** Don't give them a reason to say no. Offer something free. Offer a money-back guarantee.

f. **Evaluate Your Marketing.** Take time to review all your marketing pieces and advertising to align it with your UVP and seven-second statements. Make sure that the value and benefits for the Prospect come through clearly.

4. **Collect Information and Automate.**

a. **Set up an autoresponder system.** It may take at least seven contacts before someone does business with you. Use an autoresponder system to automatically stay in touch with your prospects.

b. **Collect e-mail addresses.** To fill your autoresponder system, use pop-ups to catch people's attention. When you start out, you'll probably have to call your current and past clients for their current e-mail address.

c. **Create an E-zine and free reports.** E-zines offer one of the easiest, most creative ways to get in front of a lot of customers on a regular basis. Develop your content and then deliver it in basic text and/or HTML format.

For a FREE 7-day course on "7 Steps To Building A Successful Marketing Plan," send an e-mail to ChipTips@ChipCummings.com

241

d. **Automate Everything.** Use a database compiling and tracking system that automates the opt-in and opt-out procedures, and is customizable for messages and import/export of data. Set up and test data collection web pages.

5. **Drive The Traffic In.**

a. **Use website addresses on *everything*.** Put it on your letterhead, brochures, business cards, advertising, notes, voice mails, invoices, statements, envelopes, etc. I mean *everything*!

b. **Research valid keywords.** Use the Overture Keyword Tool and the Google Keyword Search Tool to find out what keywords your customers are using to search for what they want.

c. **Search engine submissions.** Submit the index page of your websites to the major search engines including Google, MSN, Yahoo, and DMOZ. Either manually submit your registration to each search engine or use one of the registration services to do the job for you. To increase the odds of getting on the right search engine pages, use Google AdWords to place an ad for your website on appropriate results pages based on key words.

d. **Set up complimentary cross-links.** Work with your affiliate partners to place links on each other's websites.

e. **Use cheap e-zine or classified ads.** Advertise your free report or newsletter in online and offline periodicals.

f. **Send out Press Releases.** Publicize your free report by sending press releases to the local press.

For a FREE 7-day course on "7 Steps To Building A Successful Marketing Plan," send an e-mail to ChipTips@ChipCummings.com

242

g. **Integrate Your Other Strategies.** Make sure that other marketing strategies you are running are integrated with your on-line strategies by directing them to websites, sending e-mails, or using tools (such as payment calculators, catalogs, free gifts, etc.).

6. **Test and Track Success; is it the right kind of traffic?**

   a. **Track all your ads and website links.** Find out what's working and what's not. For example, Google AdWords provides ways to track who clicks on your links. Use different domain names for each type of marketing campaign.

   b. **Track all marketing dollars.** Test headlines, sales pages, classified ads, etc. to see which ones get the best response.

   c. **Survey customers and subscribers.** Ask your customers if it was easy for them to find you. Ask them what periodicals they read to see if these are places to advertise.

   d. **Analyze your website traffic.** Get statistics on the number of visitors, unique visitors, how long they stayed on your site, etc.

7. **Capitalize on Life-time Customer Value.**

   a. **Keep your customers happy.** A happy customer is better than a billboard. It's not just the referral value of that customer, but everyone they come in contact with. ASK them what made them happy, and what keeps them happy!

   b. **Solicit referrals immediately.** Don't wait six months to ask for referrals. Let them know that you will ask for referrals when you start working with them.

For a FREE 7-day course on "7 Steps To Building A Successful Marketing Plan," send an e-mail to ChipTips@ChipCummings.com

243

c. **Use testimonials.** Ask your customers to put their recommendation in print. Tell them you would love to share their testimonial with other customers. Ask them to write it on their letterhead or use AudioGenerator (www.InstantTalkingWebsite.com) to offer your customer's a toll-free number where they can simply call and leave an audio testimonial. Offer a "thank you" gift for giving a testimonial.

d. **Automate your "personal touches."** Chip's rule is that you need to touch your customers at least six times a year. Use autoresponders and broadcast e-mails to make this job easier.

e. **Up-sell and Package.** When possible, put similar or complimentary products together as a package, or up-sell by providing an incentive to the customer for a larger quantity or better quality. Discount multiple visits or longer-term service contracts.

Your Personal Plan of Action

Now you're ready to hit the road. To make sure you stay on the right road, concentrate on these six steps:

1. **Map out where you are going.** Plan your work and work your plan. Design a map to figure out how you are going to accomplish your goals.

2. **Focus on Past, Present and Future Customers.** Organize your plan by targeting these three groups. Each group has different wants and needs, so don't neglect one over the other. Start out stating "For past customers, I'm going to ..."

For a FREE 7-day course on "7 Steps To Building A Successful Marketing Plan," send an e-mail to ChipTips@ChipCummings.com

244

3. **Select your Marketing Strategies.** Determine what strategies you are going to use to directly reach your past, present, and future customers.

4. **Approach marketing like fishing.** It's easier to catch fish if you do the following:

   a. **Put five lines in the water.** Have at least five different marketing strategies running at any one time.

   b. **Use different bait on each line.** See what attracts each type of customer. Is it a free report? An e-zine? Professional roundtable?

   c. **Move to a new location if the fish aren't biting.** Test each method for at least 90 days, then pull your line and try somewhere else. If necessary, change the content in reports, e-zines, autoresponders, etc. (i.e. change the bait).

5. **Manage your databases.** In addition to managing your database by customer type (past, present, and future), track your database according to which type of bait is working.

6. **Educate Yourself.** Invest in yourself. Find the people who can teach you what you need to know to move up to the next level. Get a coach or a mentor. It could be somebody in your office, your business network, or outside your industry. Make a commitment to learn from people who have achieved the type of success you seek.

For a FREE 7-day course on "7 Steps To Building A Successful Marketing Plan," send an e-mail to ChipTips@ChipCummings.com

245

Above all else, enjoy what you do. There is a big difference in working for a living, and living to work. I _**truly**_ enjoy what I do. Life is too short to spend countless days dreading the tomorrows, or wondering "what could have been." You _can_ become a Top Producer. I have personally witnessed and coached hundreds of sales professionals (with little to no experience) in their determined climb to the top 5% of salespeople within their field. The systems are there. The tools are available. The formula is at your fingertips. There is only one person who controls what you decide to do now — you.

Start now. Today. Stop procrastinating, stop making excuses, and stop selling. Start listening to your market, and listening to your inner-self. Listen to the heartbeat of your success! Go Do It!

For a FREE 7-day course on "7 Steps To Building A Successful Marketing Plan," send an e-mail to ChipTips@ChipCummings.com

246

CHIP TIPS:

Here are your "personal road signs" from this Chapter:

1. Follow the seven steps to e-success.

2. Build your own personal plan of action.

3. For a FREE written 7-day mini-course on "7 Steps To Building A Successful Marketing Plan", send me a blank e-mail at ChipTips@ChipCummings.com. Then you too can witness an autoresponder series in action!

4. Last, but certainly not least — Have fun!

Best Wishes To Your Success!

For a FREE 7-day course on "7 Steps To Building A Successful Marketing Plan," send an e-mail to ChipTips@ChipCummings.com

247

DID YOU ENJOY THIS?

I hope you got a lot out of this book, and that you enjoy great success with the techniques and strategies discussed. I WANT TO HEAR FROM YOU! Send me your personal testimonial about your experience, thoughts, comments and stories. I may use your testimonial in future material, and to say thanks, I will send you a special gift for your time and comments!

Please forward your testimonial to:

Chip Cummings

Testimonials@StopSellingandStartListening.com

For a FREE 7-day course on "7 Steps To Building A Successful Marketing Plan," send an e-mail to ChipTips@ChipCummings.com

248

Chip's Million Dollar Rolodex

T he following list of resources, are companies and tools that I personally use on a regular basis for the operation of my business. If you have any problems or questions about these sites, please feel free to contact me! Best wishes to your success!

Domain Names *(search, registration, forwarding)*
   www.InstantCheapDomains.com

Website hosting *(sites, web shells)*
   www.InstantCheapDomains.com

E-zine Creation *(templates)*
   www.SimpleEzines.com

Autoresponder Systems
   www.SimpleAutoresponders.com

The Mortgage Minute *(free newsletter)*
   www.TheMortgageMinute.com

The e-Marketing Minute *(free newsletter)*
   www.TheMarketingMinute.com

Audio for websites and e-mails
   www.InstantTalkingWebsite.com

Call Capture Systems
   www.ChipCummings.com/resources.html

For a FREE 7-day course on "7 Steps To Building A Successful Marketing Plan," send an e-mail to ChipTips@ChipCummings.com

249

Copywriting — Headlines
www.ChipCummings.com/resources.html

e-Marketing 3-day Workshop
www.47MarketingSecrets.com

Chip Cummings — main website
www.ChipCummings.com

e-Marketing Conference Calls
www.AskChipCummings.com

Google Adwords
www.adwords.google.com

Alexa Toolbar
www.Alexa.com

"Good Keywords" Tool
www.goodkeywords.com

Get Your Free Report

"7 Steps to Building A Simple and Successful Marketing Plan"

Send a BLANK e-mail to:
ChipTips@ChipCummings.com

For a FREE 7-day course on "7 Steps To Building A Successful Marketing Plan," send an e-mail to ChipTips@ChipCummings.com

250

Your License For Organizational Success

This book has been formatted to follow Chip's one and two-day "Stop Selling and Start Listening" workshops that are held for companies and organizations around the country.

If you are interested in presenting this program to your sales team, company or group for meetings or workshops, there are several associated materials available including worksheets, PowerPoint presentations and leader guides.

The requirements for leaders are to personally attend one of the workshops (or conduct an on-site workshop), and provide certain written materials for each of the participants.

To find out more about conducting a live on-site interactive workshop, contact Chip Cummings Unlimited! at (616) 977-7900, via e-mail at info@ChipCummings.com, or vist www.StopSellingAndStartListening.com.

Quantity discounts of this book are available for corporations and organizations by contacting the publisher, Northwind Publishing at info@NorthwindFinancial.com.

For a FREE 7-day course on "7 Steps To Building A Successful Marketing Plan," send an e-mail to ChipTips@ChipCummings.com

251

For a FREE 7-day course on "7 Steps To Building A Successful Marketing Plan," send an e-mail to ChipTips@ChipCummings.com

252

Resources & Recommended Reading

Here are a few of the books and publications used for reference/resource material for this book which you may enjoy:

"What Clients Love" by Harry Beckwith *(Warner Books, 2003)*

"The Tipping Point" by Malcolm Gladwell *(First Back Bay, 2002)*

"Influence — Science and Practice" by Robert Cialdini *(Allyn and Bacon, 2001)*

"Jump Start Your Business Brain" by Doug Hall *(Brain Brew Books, 2001)*

"The Purple Cow" by Seth Godin *(Penguin Group, 2002)*

For a FREE 7-day course on "7 Steps To Building A Successful Marketing Plan," send an e-mail to ChipTips@ChipCummings.com

253

For a FREE 7-day course on "7 Steps To Building A Successful Marketing Plan," send an e-mail to ChipTips@ChipCummings.com

254

Tools For Success

Top Producers know that education never stops, and are aware of the need to constantly invest in themselves. Take advantage of these tools today to keep you on the "Road To Success":

Book – Stop Selling and Start Listening

Take the opportunity to pick up extra copies for friends and associates. Quantity discounts available for corporations and organizations by contacting Northwind Publishing.

Audio Book – Stop Selling and Start Listening

Listen to Chip reveal his inside secrets and thoughts in this 5-CD set complete with introduction and special bonus track – "Seven Steps To Becoming A Sales Superstar!"

8-hr. DVD Presentation – Stop Selling and Start Listening Full-Day Workshop

You've read the book, now experience the 1-day "hands-on" training workshop on this special 5-DVD set collection, complete with workshop manual and several bonus supplements.

e-Coaching Club Membership

Stay on track with monthly coaching calls, real-life strategy sessions, discounts and specials on Success Tools, preferred invitations to events and access to the "Success Network".

For a FREE 7-day course on "7 Steps To Building A Successful Marketing Plan," send an e-mail to ChipTips@ChipCummings.com

255

Personal Coaching - Consulting

Looking for specific results and Chip's personal touch? A limited number of spots are available for personal business coaching opportunities or strategic consulting. Call office to inquire regarding details and availability.

On-Site Visits & Trainings

A variety of corporate and group training sessions are available for salespeople, management teams and business organizations in ½-day, full-day, and multi-day sessions. Contact Chip Cummings Unlimited! at (616) 977-7900 for details.

Corporate events and conventions

Chip has delivered energizing presentations and keynote speeches to both large and small groups from around the world. Combining education, excitement, and experience in an entertaining presentation promises to deliver results to your next event! Call for details and availability.

Chip's Speaking Schedule

To track Chip down on the road, and hear him live and in person – check out his schedule of events and sign up for itinerary messaging (SpeakerTrack) at www.ChipCummings.com

For other "Tools For Success", visit Chip's website

at www.ChipCummings.com

For a FREE 7-day course on "7 Steps To Building A Successful Marketing Plan," send an e-mail to ChipTips@ChipCummings.com

256

Tools For Success — Order Form

To order the following products, simply fill out this form and mail with your payment information to the address listed below, or visit the "Tools For Success" section of Chip's website at www.ChipCummings.com. Thanks!

	Price	Qty.	Total
Book – Stop Selling and Start Listening	$16.95	_____	_____
Audio Book – Stop Selling and Start Listening	$69	_____	_____
DVD Presentation — **47 Marketing Secrets – Business Edition**	$997	_____	_____
e-Coaching Club Membership	$29.95 per month		_____
Sub-Total			$_____
Shipping (add $4.00 per item except Membership)			$_____
TOTAL			$_____

Guarantee: EVERYTHING we sell comes with a "no B.S." money-back lifetime guarantee. If you're not happy, SEND IT BACK!

For a FREE 7-day course on "7 Steps To Building A Successful Marketing Plan," send an e-mail to ChipTips@ChipCummings.com

257

Order Form Continued

Name: _____

Company: _____

Billing Address: _____

City: _____ State _____ Zip _____

Country _____

_____Personal Check *(made payable to Northwind Publishing)*

_____VISA _____MasterCard _____American Express

CC#_____

Expiration Date_____

Signature_____

Please send this form with your check or credit card information to:

Northwind Publishing Corporation
137 Pearl St. NW, Suite 400
Grand Rapids, MI 49503

(616) 977-7900

www.ChipCummings.com

For a FREE 7-day course on "7 Steps To Building A Successful Marketing Plan," send an e-mail to ChipTips@ChipCummings.com

258

Tools For Success — Order Form

To order the following products, simply fill out this form and mail with your payment information to the address listed below, or visit the "Tools For Success" section of Chip's website at www.ChipCummings.com. Thanks!

	Price	Qty.	Total
Book – Stop Selling and Start Listening	$16.95	_____	_____
Audio Book – Stop Selling and Start Listening	$69	_____	_____
DVD Presentation — **47 Marketing Secrets – Business Edition**	$997	_____	_____
e-Coaching Club Membership	$29.95 per month		_____

Sub-Total $_____

Shipping (add $4.00 per item except Membership) $_____

TOTAL $_____

Guarantee: EVERYTHING we sell comes with a
"no B.S." money-back lifetime guarantee. If
you're not happy, SEND IT BACK!

For a FREE 7-day course on "7 Steps To Building A Successful Marketing Plan," send an e-mail to ChipTips@ChipCummings.com

259

Order Form Continued

Name: _____

Company: _____

Billing Address: _____

City: _____ State _____ Zip _____

Country _____

_____Personal Check *(made payable to Northwind Publishing)*

_____VISA _____MasterCard _____American Express

CC#_____

Expiration Date_____

Signature_____

Please send this form with your check or credit card information to:

Northwind Publishing Corporation
137 Pearl St. NW, Suite 400
Grand Rapids, MI 49503

(616) 977-7900

www.ChipCummings.com

For a FREE 7-day course on "7 Steps To Building A Successful Marketing Plan," send an e-mail to ChipTips@ChipCummings.com

260

About The Author

Chip entered the world of sales at age 9, selling rocks and candy to neighborhood kids in his hometown of Rye, New York. After relocating to Ann Arbor, Michigan at age 12, Chip started his first business, an entertainment sound and lighting production company before he turned 16, and then sold it a few years later. He entertained as a disc jockey, and worked on concert tours while finding time to attend Eastern Michigan University. Having worked part-time in a real estate office throughout high school, he also went on to work for several real estate sales and development firms, and moved into the world of finance at the age of 20.

Chip has started over 30 different companies, and accumulated over one billion dollars in sales volume. For the last several years, Chip has dedicated his time to training, educating, and speaking to sales professionals all over the world, working with many major organizations including the National Association of Mortgage Brokers, AT&T, First American Corporation, Flagstar Bank, and Ellie Mae. He has served as President of the Michigan Mortgage Brokers Association, been a member of numerous state and national boards and committees, and is the recipient of several awards.

For a FREE 7-day course on "7 Steps To Building A Successful Marketing Plan," send an e-mail to ChipTips@ChipCummings.com

261

In addition to designing several training programs, he has published dozens of articles.

During his free time (when not traveling), you can find him on the golf course, in the water, or playing with his kids. Chip is most proud to be the "Dad" to Katelyn, C.J. and Joe, and resides in Rockford, Michigan with his wife Lisa.

For a FREE 7-day course on "7 Steps To Building A Successful Marketing Plan," send an e-mail to ChipTips@ChipCummings.com

262